Resilient Recovery Workbook

Jason Jonker

DEDICATION

"For the aching ones whose wounds cannot be nursed
For the countless confused, accused, misused, strung-out ones an' worse
And for every hung-up person in the whole wide universe."

Bob Dylan

Contents

ACKNOWLEDGMENTS

I'd like to acknowledge my muses: the brothers and sisters in treatment here in Laveen, AZ. You have every right to have kept your story to yourself. But you chose to share with me and the group. This book would have been superficial without your input and feedback in every group session.

I also can't pass up the opportunity to thank Pastor Dan Solofra for patiently teaching me to parse the law from the gospel. You don't remember it, but your comments after a group many years ago changed the format of these group sessions and the course of my life for eternity. Thanks for all your support and guidance!

FREQUENTLY ASKED QUESTIONS

Welcome to this Resilient Recovery Group. We are glad you are here. Our goal is to take away confusion and give you a clear understanding of what to expect in a Resilient Recovery Group.

1. **Who are these groups for?** This group is for anyone who is considering making a change in their drinking and drug use. We also welcome people who have other addictions. We also appreciate those who come to Resilient Recovery Groups to support a friend or family member with an addiction.

2. **What happens here?** When new people attend, people with more experience in the program will introduce themselves and share why they come to Resilient. In the meeting, a facilitator will guide us through a lesson. Volunteers will read brief sections of writing. The facilitator will ask a couple of questions, and volunteers will answer the questions.

3. **Do I have to talk?** No one has to talk, read, introduce themselves, or respond to questions. Just say, "I pass." Passing is perfectly OK. We're glad you are here.

4. **How long will the meeting last?** The meeting lasts about an hour. The facilitator or someone else may use a timer to keep the group on track. This makes sure everyone who wants to participate can participate—and that we get out of the meeting on time.

5. **Is this like Alcoholics Anonymous?** Resilient Recovery Groups are different from AA. Our groups are Christian. So, our practices are based on the Bible, and we use scripture in our meetings. Instead of the 12 steps, we encourage the Biblical practice of confession and forgiveness. We speak openly about God and Jesus, which is sometimes not acceptable in an AA meeting.

6. **Is this like Celebrate Recovery?** Resilient Recovery Groups have a different meeting structure, and unlike CR, we do not use the 12 steps. We also do not believe a person decides to become a believer. Instead, we emphasize the grace and mercy of God in giving us the gift of faith. For more information about our beliefs, check out "GotQuestions.org."

7. **Are you against AA and CR?** No. We are not against anything that helps people get sober. And we believe that God uses both AA and CR to bring people to faith and sobriety.

8. **Do I have to be Christian to attend?** No. We welcome people of other faiths and of no faith at all. We also encourage you to share your beliefs, no matter what those beliefs are. Yes, you will hear a clear Christian message from the lesson and some of the group members. But we won't force our beliefs. We think God has given wisdom and insight to all his creatures. So, we are interested in your thoughts.

More Questions? Contact us via email: Resilient@cwlk.church

HOW IT WORKS

Addiction causes a shame cycle.

But confession and belief in God's forgiveness give us hope and motivation.

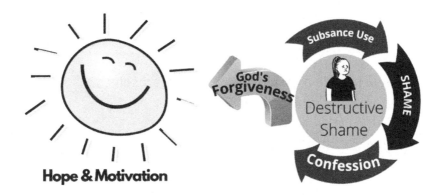

NEW PERSON CHECKLIST

SCAN ME

☐ Facilitator introduces self

☐ Show explainer video (Scan the QR code for the video)

☐ Call meeting to order with a prayer

☐ Review The Group Sharing Guidelines

☐ Review the Resilient Acrostic

☐ Ask people to briefly introduce themselves and share why they are here

☐ Follow steps in lesson

☐ Pass out communication cards

☐ Closing announcements

☐ Close with Prayer

GROUP SHARING GUIDELINES

Twice you'll be asked if you want to respond to questions from the lesson. These guidelines will help make sure that the sharing of responses is helpful and orderly.

CONFIDENTIALITY

What is said in Resilient—and who comes to Resilient—stays in Resilient. The physical safety of a person is the only reason to break confidentiality. Even then, there are limits on what is shared.

AVOID CROSSTALKING

Please don't have side conversations. Instead, give each speaker your full attention.

SPEAK FROM EXPERIENCE

Talk about yourself, not others. Please don't interrupt, correct, or give advice.

SHARE THE FLOOR

Your thoughts and life experiences will help someone else. But do not dominate the conversation.

USE OF A TIMER

We often use a timer to help us end on time. When you hear the timer, you do not need to stop talking immediately. But it is time to wrap up, and not time to start a new line of thought.

PRAY

We pause to pray if somebody is sharing something difficult or they express overwhelming fear, anger, or hopelessness.

SHARE EVEN PARTIAL THOUGHTS

We ask difficult questions. Sometimes you are not sure what to say or what answer to give to a question. It's ok to think out loud or share incomplete thoughts.

THE RESILIENT ACROSTIC

The Resilient acrostic is a series of sentences that begin with the first letter of the word "Resilient." Many of us have found the Resilient acrostic to be a simple way to remember Biblical truths that apply to recovery.

R - Rest in Jesus and his Promises

E - Express My Need for Jesus

S - Seek God's Presence and Power

I - Imagine Freedom in Christ

L - Live Transparently by Owning My Sin

I - Invite Jesus to Change Me

E - Exalt Jesus above All Things

N - Neutralize Temptation through Meditation on God's Word

T - Tell Others What God Has Done for You

STOP CARRYING A HEAVY LOAD.

Reader 1: (Scripture)

⁵"*Yes, I must find my rest in God.*
He is the God who gives me hope.
⁶ *It is surely true that he is my rock and the God who saves me.*
He is like a fort to me, so I will always be secure.
⁷ *I depend on God to save me and to honor me.*
He is my mighty rock and my place of safety.[Psalm 62:5-7]"

Reader 2: Are you feeling tired of the problems, heavy loads, and frustrations in your life? Do you wish you could get a break? Maybe you are tired of hearing another person criticize you. Tired of yourself. Tired of the legal system. Tired of trying and failing. Tired of feeling tired.

Rosie felt tired of all the above. Sometimes she felt weighed down by everything that was going on in her life. But unlike the writer of the psalm, she did not turn to God when she was tired of things. She did not trust him or believe that he would help. Instead, she turned to drugs and alcohol. She liked how they made her feel—even though she knew they were only temporary solutions and that she felt more tired and overwhelmed afterward.

Facilitator Questions

Did you turn to alcohol and drugs when you were tired, carrying a heavy load, or dealing with problems?

_____
_____
_____

Did drugs and alcohol make the problem better or worse?

_____
_____
_____

Reader 3: We have meditated on the law and confessed that we turned to drugs and alcohol for what only God could give us. We also confessed that the results of turning to drugs and alcohol were not good. Let us take a moment to continue that confession in personal, silent prayer.

Reader 4: (Announcement of forgiveness, grace, and mercy) Jesus had many reasons to feel like he was carrying a heavy load. He could easily have decided he was fed up, overwhelmed, and tired of this world and the people in it. Yet he did not give up on the world or on us. In fact, he works hard in order to offer us rest.

> [28]"Come to me, all you who are tired and are carrying heavy loads. I will give you rest. [29]Become my servants and learn from me. I am gentle and free of pride. You will find rest for your souls. [30] Serving me is easy, and my load is light." [Matthew 11:28-30]

When Jesus died on the cross, he took our heavy load so we will never need to carry it again. The weight of our shame and guilt was placed on his shoulders so that it could be lifted from ours. For his sake, God forgives our sins and calls us from darkness to his marvelous light. Therefore, I forgive you all your sins and I give all your guilt, regret, and shame to Christ in the name of the Father and of the Son and of the Holy Spirit.

Everyone: Amen.

Facilitator Questions

What does Jesus mean when he says serving him is easy and his load is light?

_____

_____

_____

When you face troubles, what helps lighten the load?

_____

_____

_____

YOU CAN BECOME GREAT

Reader 1: (Scripture)

[1]"At that time the disciples came to Jesus. They asked him, "Then who is the most important person in the kingdom of heaven?"

[2] Jesus called a little child over to him. He had the child stand among them. [3] Jesus said, "What I'm about to tell you is true. You need to change and become like little children. If you don't, you will never enter the kingdom of heaven. [4] Anyone who takes the humble position of this child is the most important in the kingdom of heaven. [5] Anyone who welcomes a little child like this one in my name welcomes me." [Matthew 18:1-5]

Reader 2: Drugs and alcohol made Kenny feel like a grown man. When he bought a bottle for his friends, he felt important and well-liked. When he drank, he got loud and fearless, which made him feel tough and respected. He was proud that he could drink more than other people. He thought it was weak not to drink. He didn't want anyone to laugh at him or say, "you probably can't do a shot of this!"

His friend Shelly also thought alcohol and drugs were part of being a grown-up. She thought drinking wine was sophisticated and fancy. After a hard day of working and raising kids, she felt like she deserved an adult beverage. Sometimes, she also did drugs to relax and have a little fun. She didn't like it when her family talked about her drinking. She'd say, "I am a grown woman. You can't tell me what to do!"

Neither Kenny nor Shelly wanted to admit they needed to become like little children to get sober.

Facilitator Questions

Did you associate drinking and drug use with being grown-up, respected, tough, sophisticated, or powerful?

_____

_____

_____

When you were drinking or using drugs, were you proud of things that you should not have been?

_____

_____

_____

Reader 3: We have confessed that we thought alcohol and drugs would make us grown-up, respected, tough, or powerful. We have also confessed that we were proud of things we should not have been proud of. Let's take a moment to continue that confession in personal silent prayer.

Reader 4: (Announcement of forgiveness, grace, and mercy) It's ok that we are like little children. God loves children.

> *10-11 "See that you don't look down on one of these little ones. Here is what I tell you. Their angels in heaven are always with my Father who is in heaven.*

> *12 "What do you think? Suppose a man owns 100 sheep and one of them wanders away. Won't he leave the 99 sheep on the hills? Won't he go and look for the one that wandered off? 13 What I'm about to tell you is true. If he finds that sheep, he is happier about the one than about the 99 that didn't wander off. 14 It is the same with your Father in heaven. He does not want any of these little ones to die." [Matthew 18:11-14]*

Jesus doesn't want any of us to die. So, he humbled himself when we did not. He became a little child. He went even lower and became despised and hated by this world. He then lowered himself even more, taking the lowest position in history. He became a sacrifice to pay for our worst sin and shame. By lowering himself, he has made it possible for us to be lifted up. Because of his descent into hell, we will be lifted up to heaven. Therefore, I forgive you all your sins in the name of the Father and of the Son and of the Holy Spirit.

Everyone: Amen.

Facilitator Questions

What qualities do children have that we adults should try to get back?

_____
_____
_____

What makes someone great?

_____
_____
_____

DO YOU NEED ANYTHING?

Reader 1: *(Scripture)*

⁷LORD, hear my voice when I call out to you.
Treat me with kindness and answer me.

⁸ My heart says, "Seek him!"
LORD, I will seek you.

⁹Don't turn your face away from me.
Don't turn me away because you are angry.
You have helped me.
God my Savior, don't say no to me.
Don't desert me.

¹⁰ My father and mother may desert me,
but the LORD will accept me. *[Psalm 27:7-10]*

Reader 2: John didn't like to ask for help. He was sure people looked down on him for needing help. He thought people talked about him, spreading rumors and gossip. So, he concluded it was easier to figure things out on his own than to ask for help.

Sometimes John thought it was wrong to ask for help. He thought people needed to take care of their own problems. He'd say, "I did this to myself; so, I can take the consequences, too."

John also hated to let others think he was weak. He'd rather stay stuck in his problems than admit he needed help.

Because John wouldn't ask for help, his addiction got worse.

Facilitator Questions

What led you to ask for help?

_____
_____
_____

What has been the cost of not asking for help earlier?

_____
_____
_____

Reader 3: We have confessed our sins to God and to each other. We confessed that we needed help and that there was a cost for not asking for help earlier. Let's take a moment to continue that confession in personal, silent prayer.

Reader 4: (Announcement of forgiveness, grace, and mercy) Jesus is willing to help anyone who asks. His mission on earth was a mission to save and set people free. He tells us:

> [1] *The Spirit of the Lord and King is on me.*
> *The Lord has anointed me*
> *to announce good news to poor people.*
> *He has sent me to comfort*
> *those whose hearts have been broken.*
> *He has sent me to announce freedom*
> *for those who have been captured.*
> *He wants me to set prisoners free*
> *from their dark cells.*
>
> [2] *He has sent me to announce the year*
> *when he will set his people free." [Isaiah 61:1-2 (Luke 4:18-19)]*

There is no reason for us to avoid Jesus when we need anything. His words and actions made it clear that he cares about people who need help. In his life on earth, Jesus was on a mission to save the poor, the broken-hearted, the prisoners, and the oppressed. His body still bears the scars, and his hands still have the holes from the nails that held him to the cross. These are evidence of his earnest desire to help. For his sake, God forgives our sins and hears our cries for help. Therefore, I forgive you all your sins in the name of the Father and of the Son and of the Holy Spirit.

Everyone: Amen.

Facilitator Questions

If you asked for help from Jesus, do you think he would treat you with respect and compassion?

_____
_____
_____

What do you need help with?

_____
_____
_____

NOT HAPPY?

Reader 1: (Scripture) *⁴Always be joyful because you belong to the Lord. I will say it again. Be joyful! ⁵Let everyone know how gentle you are. The Lord is coming soon. ⁶Don't worry about anything. No matter what happens, tell God about everything. Ask and pray, and give thanks to him. ⁷Then God's peace will watch over your hearts and your minds. He will do this because you belong to Christ Jesus. God's peace can never be completely understood. [Philippians 4:4-7]*

Reader 2: Sedrick was not joyful, and he wasn't filled with peace. In fact, he was often upset, and he complained all the time. If you tape-recorded Sedrick's thoughts, you would hear a stream of cursing and swearing. Sometimes his complaints were aimed at other people. Sometimes his complaints were aimed at objects. Sometimes he cursed and swore at himself. There were even times when he complained about God.

Sedrick drank and used drugs when he wanted to feel happier. Yet his life was getting more and more unhappy.

His addiction robbed him of peace. Hangovers made him irritable and sick. Conflicts with his family made him miserable and isolated. He got kicked out of places. His work life suffered. And he never seemed to have enough money.

Facilitator Questions

Have drugs and alcohol made you happier?

_____

_____

_____

Did drinking and drugs give you peace?

_____

_____

_____

Reader 3: We have confessed our sins to God and to each other. We have confessed that drugs and alcohol didn't bring us peace or happiness. Let's take a moment to continue that confession in personal, silent prayer.

Reader 4: (Announcement of forgiveness, grace and mercy) Jesus had a peace that can never be completely understood. He refused to complain despite being beaten, mocked, and convicted of a crime he did not commit. Even as he was dying on the cross, he asked the Father to forgive the people who were killing him. In all ways possible, he displayed the fruit that the Holy Spirit produces.

22 [. . .] the fruit the Holy Spirit produces is love, joy and peace. It is being patient, kind and good. It is being faithful 23 and gentle and having control of oneself. There is no law against things of that kind. 24 Those who belong to Christ Jesus have nailed their sinful desires to his cross. They don't want these things anymore. 25 Since we live by the Spirit, let us keep in step with the Spirit. [Galatians 5:22-25]

We can belong to Jesus and have his peace. We can nail our sins to the cross where they can die. With our sins nailed to the cross, we can live spiritually from now on. The Holy Spirit can produce fruit of love, joy, and peace. We can become kind, patient, and good. We can be faithful and gentle—and we can have self-control. Therefore, I forgive you all your sins in the name of the Father and of the Son and of the Holy Spirit.

Everyone: Amen.

Facilitator Questions

What brings you love, joy, and peace?

_____

_____

_____

Now that your sins are nailed to the cross, what kind of person do you want God's help to become?

_____

_____

_____

ESCAPE FROM IT ALL

Reader 1: (Scripture)

> [4] *I'm asking the Lord for only one thing.*
> *Here is what I want.*
> *I want to live in the house of the Lord*
> *all the days of my life.*
> *I want to look at the beauty of the Lord.*
> *I want to worship him in his temple. [Psalm 27:4]*

Reader 2: Benny was looking for an escape. The pain of a recent loss was overwhelming. So, he turned to alcohol and drugs to get a break from his sadness and grief. When bills piled up, people were mad at him, or someone treated him badly, he felt he could not face the problem. Instead, he wanted to get away and not think about his difficulties.

Benny longed for peace, and he looked for it in substances. He desired joy, and he tried to find it in partying. He wanted to feel nothing, and he numbed himself with alcohol and drugs.

Benny thought it was strange to find an escape by worshiping the LORD. He didn't understand how reading the Bible, singing, and praying could transport him out of his troubles and give him a break from difficulties.

So, Benny continued to use substances to escape for the moment, but he was left empty and unsatisfied. Instead of improving his life, he felt sicker, poorer, or more unhappy than before he indulged.

Facilitator Questions

Did you turn to drugs and alcohol for an escape?

_____

_____

_____

Was the escape that alcohol and drugs gave you a good one?

_____

_____

_____

Reader 3: We have confessed our sins to God and to each other. Turning to drugs and alcohol for an escape was a mistake. Let's take a moment to continue that confession in personal, silent prayer.

Reader 4: (Announcement of forgiveness, grace, and mercy) Jesus would often escape the crowds and go to a private place to pray. It was his way of resting and recharging. But when it came to facing Hell for us, he chose not to escape. He stuck with the experience of suffering all the way through his crucifixion and death. He got no relief or escape from it. He did this so we could be saved from the suffering that we deserve because of our sins. He suffered so we could have our suffering relieved here on earth (in part) and in heaven (completely). On the cross, he was ejected from God's presence so we could enter it.

> [3] *The Son is the shining brightness of God's glory. He is the exact likeness of God's being. He uses his powerful word to hold all things together. He provided the way for people to be made pure from sin. Then he sat down at the right hand of the King, the Majesty in heaven.* [Hebrews 1:3]

For his sake, God forgives our sins and allows us to experience the presence and power of God. Therefore, I forgive you all your sins in the name of the Father and of the Son and of the Holy Spirit.

Everyone: Amen.

Facilitator Questions

What will it feel like to escape this earth and enter heaven?

_____

_____

_____

What are some God-pleasing ways to get away and recharge?

_____

_____

_____

FULLY ACCEPTED

Reader 1: (Scripture) *16 I pray that he will use his glorious riches to make you strong. May his Holy Spirit give you his power deep down inside you. 17 Then Christ will live in your hearts because you believe in him. And I pray that your love will have deep roots. I pray that it will have a strong foundation. 18 May you have power together with all the Lord's holy people to understand Christ's love. May you know how wide and long and high and deep it is. 19 And may you know his love, even though it can't be known completely. Then you will be filled with everything God has for you. [Ephesians 3:16-19]*

Reader 2: Joanna felt empty and insecure. She wanted to be liked and she wanted to fit in. She didn't want to feel alone.

She liked how drinking and drugs made her feel. They were like a hug for her brain, letting her know everything was ok, and she was lovable.

She also liked a party. She enjoyed the noise and laughter of the big group. She also enjoyed "deep conversations" with smaller groups of people—or even a one-on-one talk with a close friend or a guy.

But parties never last. And in the end, Joanna was increasingly isolated and alone. She often felt depressed, which made the next party sound like a great way to escape her bad mood.

Facilitator Questions

Did you turn to alcohol and drugs to avoid loneliness and insecurity?

_____
_____
_____

Was turning to alcohol and drugs helpful or harmful to your social life?

_____
_____
_____

Reader 3: We have confessed our sins to God and to each other. We admitted that we turned to drugs and alcohol to solve the problem of loneliness and insecurity and that our social life was harmed. Let's take a moment to continue that confession in personal, silent prayer.

Reader 4: (Announcement of forgiveness, grace, and mercy) Jesus offers us deep and unconditional love.

> [15] *The Spirit you received doesn't make you slaves. Otherwise you would live in fear again. Instead, the Holy Spirit you received made you God's adopted child. By the Spirit's power we call God Abba. Abba means Father.* [16] *The Spirit himself joins with our spirits. Together they tell us that we are God's children.* [17] *As his children, we will receive all that he has for us. We will share what Christ receives. But we must share in his sufferings if we want to share in his glory." [Romans 8:15-17]*

We may suffer some rejection here on earth from people who don't want to see us succeed. We may also experience anger and rejection from people who aren't ready to forgive us. And there are people who want to pull us down into addiction again. But God does not reject us or try to pull us down. He wants us to be his children, and give us a home and family that accepts us completely. Therefore, I forgive you all your sins in the name of the Father and of the Son and of the Holy Spirit.

Everyone: Amen.

Facilitator Questions

What is true love for another human being?

_____

_____

_____

Could the love of God help you stay sober?

_____

_____

_____

BEAT BAD MOODS

Reader 1: (Scripture)¹⁹ *My dear friends, don't try to get even. Leave room for God to show his anger. It is written, "I am the God who judges people. I will pay them back," says the Lord. ²⁰ Do just the opposite. Scripture says,*

> *"If your enemies are hungry, give them food to eat.*
> *If they are thirsty, give them something to drink.*
> *By doing those things, you will pile up burning coals on their heads."*

²¹ Don't let evil overcome you. Overcome evil by doing good. [Romans 12:19-21]

Reader 2: Things that people do or circumstances we do not like, can put us in a bad mood. That bad mood is called resentment and resentment can make us slaves. Resentment forces us to do things like:

- Think about the source of the resentment, even when you do not want to.
- Pout and sulk instead of quickly forgiving.
- Reject calls, gifts, or invitations to get-togethers and celebrations from people or places we resent.
- Rejoice in the suffering of a person or place because they "deserve it."
- Feel that we deserve to get drunk or high because we're mad.
- Think, "If that is how they are going to act, I'm going to drink or use drugs."

Forgiveness frees us from resentment.

And forgiveness puts us back in the right relationship with God. It is God's job—not ours—to repay. Forgiveness lets God be God and removes us from his throne of judgment.

Facilitator Questions

What puts you in a bad mood?

_____

_____

_____

Has resentment contributed to your drinking and drug use? How?

_____

_____

_____

Reader 3: We have confessed our sins to God and to each other. We've admitted we get resentful and that resentment has contributed to our drinking and drug use. Let's take a moment to continue that confession in personal, silent prayer.

Reader 4: (Announcement of forgiveness, grace, and mercy) God is not resentful toward us. He does not feel inconvenienced or taken advantage of by our neediness. He lets things go instead of holding grudges. He forgives us generously; he is ready to forgive no matter how many times we have already been forgiven.

> *[6] All those things bring praise to his glorious grace. God freely gave us his grace because of the One he loves. [7] We have been set free because of what Christ has done. Because he bled and died our sins have been forgiven. We have been set free because God's grace is so rich. [8] He poured his grace on us. [Ephesians 1:6-8]*

Because of Christ, God forgives our sins and calls us from slavery to resentment to the freedom of love and forgiveness. Therefore, I forgive you all your sins in the name of the Father and of the Son and of the Holy Spirit.

Everyone: Amen.

Facilitator Questions

What are some examples of God's grace in your life?

_____

_____

_____

Have you ever forgiven someone? Tell us a little about that.

_____

_____

_____

LOSE YOUR LIFE

Reader 1: (Scripture) _23Then he said to all of them, "Whoever wants to follow me must say no to themselves. They must pick up their cross every day and follow me. 24 Whoever wants to save their life will lose it. But whoever loses their life for me will save it. 25 What good is it if someone gains the whole world but loses or gives up their very self?_ [Luke 9:23-25]

Reader 2: Catherine thought saying "No" to herself was dumb. In Catherine's mind, life was short, and life was often unfair. So why shouldn't she have a little fun and relaxation when she could?

She said "Yes" to herself any time she wanted to drink or use drugs. And she never said "No" to people, places, or things that led to getting high. "Why should I have to give those things up, just to stay sober?"

Catherine was also avoiding taking care of important tasks because she didn't want to do them. She thought that doing these tasks would be stressful and boring. So, she stalled and delayed when it came to taking care of legal paperwork, filing taxes, paying bills, and other important tasks. Rather than take care of these tasks, she would drink or use drugs.

Catherine didn't realize that everyone has crosses they must carry in life, that is, they have difficult and stressful things they have to do. She also didn't know that it's wiser to say "No" to yourself and take care of stressful and boring tasks.

Although she couldn't see it, the more she tried to enjoy herself, the worse she felt. The more she delayed taking care of important tasks, the more stressed she got.

Facilitator Questions

When you were drinking and using drugs, did you say "Yes" to yourself too often?

_____

_____

_____

Did you stall or delay doing important tasks?

_____

_____

_____

Reader 3: We've confessed to God and to each other that we said "yes" to ourselves too often. We've also confessed that we have delayed doing important tasks. Let's take a moment to continue our confession in personal, silent prayer.

Reader 4: (Announcement of forgiveness, grace, and mercy) God wants to teach us how to say no to ourselves. He wants to show us how to do what is right, even when it is stressful or boring.

> *[11] God's grace has now appeared. By his grace, God offers to save all people. [12] His grace teaches us to say no to godless ways and sinful desires. We must control ourselves. We must do what is right. We must lead godly lives in today's world. [13] That's how we should live as we wait for the blessed hope God has given us. We are waiting for Jesus Christ to appear in his glory. He is our great God and Savior. [14] He gave himself for us. By doing that, he set us free from all evil. He wanted to make us pure. He wanted us to be his very own people. He wanted us to desire to do what is good. [Titus 2:11-14]*

It's interesting that God gives us gifts to help us say no to ourselves and to show us how to do what is right. God is a good and kind teacher. For example, God's grace—not his anger or judgment—teaches us to say no. The gift of hope can help us lead godly lives in today's world. The promise that we will see Jesus helps us wait with patience. Therefore, I forgive you all your sins in the name of the Father and of the Son and of the Holy Spirit.

Everyone: Amen.

Facilitator Questions

What are you saying "No" to that you weren't in the past?

_____

_____

_____

How can God-given hope and dreams help you do what is right and stay sober?

_____

_____

_____

BE A DOER

Reader 1: (Scripture) *22 Don't just listen to the word. You fool yourselves if you do that. You must do what it says. 23 Suppose someone listens to the word but doesn't do what it says. Then they are like a person who looks at their face in a mirror. 24 After looking at themselves, they leave. And right away they forget what they look like. 25 But suppose someone takes a good look at the perfect law that gives freedom. And they keep looking at it. Suppose they don't forget what they've heard, but they do what the law says. Then this person will be blessed in what they do.* [James 1:22-25]

Reader 2: Rick knew he needed to make a change long before he asked for help. To his credit, he did make some attempts to change. But they were very small attempts to control his use. And things just kept getting worse in terms of his health, his relationships, and his legal situation.

Rick needed to take real action. Good intentions and great ideas did not do him any good until he put them into practice.

One day Rick got sick of everything and decided to take a step forward. He was nervous. He felt embarrassed. He was ashamed that it took him so long to get started. But he pushed all those negative thoughts aside and took a small step forward.

It was not easy. But 5 years of sobriety later, the only thing he regretted was not getting sober earlier.

Facilitator Questions

Were you a doer of God's Word when you were drinking and using drugs?

_____

_____

_____

Is there a step forward that you need to stop procrastinating about?

_____

_____

_____

Reader 3: We have confessed to God and to each other that did not do what the Word of God commanded when we were drinking and using drugs. And we have also confessed there is a step now we need to stop procrastinating about. Let's take a moment to continue our confession in personal, silent prayer.

Reader 4: (Announcement of forgiveness, grace, and mercy) Jesus is the Supreme Doer of the Word. His actions during his life on earth are the perfect example of doing what the Word says to do. But Jesus did more than be an example. He paid for all the times we were "hearers only" and not doers of the Word.

> [24] *"He himself carried our sins" in his body on the cross. He did it so that we would die as far as sins are concerned. Then we would lead godly lives. "His wounds have healed you." [1 Peter 2:24]*

Jesus suffered greatly to pay for our sins. No one in history has been so unselfish and so kind. Even when he was accused and persecuted, he continued to love and sacrifice for us. In every way possible, he was a doer of the Word.

> [6] *In his very nature he was God.*
> *Jesus was equal with God. But Jesus didn't take advantage of that fact.*
>
> [7] *Instead, he made himself nothing.*
> *He did this by taking on the nature of a servant.*
> *He was made just like human beings.*
>
> [8] *He appeared as a man.*
> *He was humble and obeyed God completely. He did this even though it led to his death.*
> *Even worse, he died on a cross! [Philippians 2:6-8]*

No one will ever reach the perfection of Jesus in this life. But through faith, our sins are forgiven, and Jesus' record of perfection is transferred to our account. Therefore, I forgive you all your sins in the name of the Father and of the Son and of the Holy Spirit.

Everyone: Amen.

Facilitator Questions

If there is a step that you need to take in your recovery now, what can you do to get started?

_____

_____

_____

What qualities or actions of Jesus would you like to be able to put into practice?

_____

_____

_____

STOP HUSTLING

Reader 1: (Scripture) *⁸ Pay everything you owe. But you can never pay back all the love you owe one another. Whoever loves other people has done everything the law requires. ⁹ Here are some commandments to think about. "Do not commit adultery." "Do not commit murder." "Do not steal." "Do not want what belongs to others." These and all other commands are included in one command. Here's what it is. "Love your neighbor as you love yourself." ¹⁰ Love does not harm its neighbor. So love does everything the law requires. [Romans 13:8-10]*

Reader 2: Ronald did not consider himself homeless. Homeless was a word that sounded weak and inactive. Ronald saw himself as a hustler. He hustled to survive and get what he needed. Sometimes that meant doing a quick job here and there. Sometimes it meant asking for a few dollars, a ride, or a place to stay. Sometimes it meant doing something questionable to earn money. But it always involved presenting himself in a way that gained sympathy or got cooperation from others. He often kept information to himself so he would have the upper hand.

Most of the time Ronald didn't see how his hustling hurt other people. But sometimes he did. In those times, he knew he was manipulating people to get what he needed to keep using. At his core, he knew he was loving himself and his addiction more than the people he was hustling.

Facilitator Questions

What are some ways you hustled, took advantage of, or manipulated people?

_____

_____

_____

Share some ways that you cheated people out of what was rightful theirs.

_____

_____

_____

Reader 3: We have confessed our sins to God and to each other. We've confessed that we have not loved others as we should. Let's take a moment to continue our reflection in silence by going to God and confessing our times that did not love our neighbor as ourselves (btw, everyone we have contact with is our neighbor).

Reader 4: (Announcement of forgiveness, grace, and mercy) Jesus is the exact opposite of a hustler and manipulator. Instead of trying to score some quick cash for himself, Jesus poured himself out for the benefit of others. His greatest act of love was to die for our sins.

> ¹³ *No one has greater love than the one who gives their life for their friends.* ¹⁴ *You are my friends if you do what I command.* ¹⁵ *I do not call you slaves anymore. Slaves do not know their master's business. Instead, I have called you friends. I have told you everything I learned from my Father.* ¹⁶ *You did not choose me. Instead, I chose you. I appointed you so that you might go and bear fruit that will last. I also appointed you so that the Father will give you what you ask for. He will give you whatever you ask for in my name.* ¹⁷ *Here is my command. Love one another.* [John 15:13-17]

Notice also that Jesus doesn't hide his true intent from us. He shares everything his Father taught him. He holds nothing back for himself. By sharing everything, he treats us like true friends.

Before Christ, we were slaves to ourselves and our addiction. His love makes us free to do things for other people, not ourselves. He calls it "bearing fruit" when we love others as we love ourselves. Bearing fruit is healthy, enjoyable, and life-giving.

Because of Christ's unselfish love for us, I forgive you all your sins in the name of the Father and of the Son and of the Holy Spirit.

Everyone: Amen.

Facilitator Questions

How do you feel when you do things for other people?

_____

_____

_____

Knowing that you are loved and forgiven by Jesus, how can you show love to others?

_____

_____

_____

GOD PROVIDES AN ESCAPE

Reader 1: (Scripture) *¹³ You are tempted in the same way all other human beings are. God is faithful. He will not let you be tempted any more than you can take. But when you are tempted, God will give you a way out. Then you will be able to deal with it.* [1 Corinthians 10:13]

Reader 2: To Julius, the temptation to use seemed overwhelming. Twice he left his treatment to go back on the street and use.

During the last 10 years of drug abuse, he burned bridges, lost jobs, and failed to take advantage of the help that was offered to him. He had been arrested and his health was in jeopardy.

But nothing he tried seemed to be more powerful than the temptation to use drugs.

Julius didn't want to admit that when he was tempted, God gave him "a way out." The way out might be people, strategies, and support to help him overcome addiction. To stay sober, he will have to be honest about his temptation and use the way out that God gives him.

Facilitator Questions

Were there chances and opportunities to get sober that you didn't take?

_____

_____

_____

What people, strategies, and support do you need to take advantage of to stay sober in the future?

_____

_____

_____

Reader 3: We've confessed our sins to God and to each other. We've confessed that we needed a way out of addiction and that we will need to continue to work at sobriety. Let's take a moment to continue our confession in personal silent prayer.

Reader 4: (Announcement of forgiveness, grace, and mercy) The night he was turned over to the authorities to be crucified, Jesus battled with temptation. He was tempted to back out of the crucifixion. He reached out for help.

> *36 Then Jesus went with his disciples to a place called Gethsemane. He said to them, "Sit here while I go over there and pray." 37 He took Peter and the two sons of Zebedee along with him. He began to be sad and troubled. 38 Then he said to them, "My soul is very sad. I feel close to death. Stay here. Keep watch with me."*
>
> *39 He went a little farther. Then he fell with his face to the ground. He prayed, "My Father, if it is possible, take this cup of suffering away from me. But let what you want be done, not what I want." [Matthew 26:36-39]*

In this verse, Jesus provides a great example to us. He doesn't hide the fact that he is tempted. Nor does he minimize the amount of that temptation. Instead, he makes it clear how deeply he is being tempted and asks for support. Telling others about temptation and asking for support are great strategies to deal with temptation.

But even more important than the example Jesus sets is the fact that Jesus succeeded at resisting temptation when we couldn't. His success at resisting temptation means that you and I can be forgiven for our failures. Because of his strength and endurance, our weakness and stumbling are wiped away. His triumph over temptation is greater than all our defeats.

Because Jesus did not give into temptation, all our sins and failures are forgiven. Therefore, I forgive you all your sins in the name of the Father and of the Son and of the Holy Spirit.

Everyone: Amen.

Facilitator Questions

Does being completely forgiven—being certain of the fact that all guilt and shame are gone—make it easier or harder to overcome temptation?

_____
_____
_____

What "way out" of temptation will you use the next time you are tempted?

_____
_____
_____

MOTIVATED BY JOY

Reader 1: (Scripture) [1]. . .*So let us throw off everything that stands in our way. Let us throw off any sin that holds on to us so tightly. And let us keep on running the race marked out for us.* [2] *Let us keep looking to Jesus. He is the one who started this journey of faith. And he is the one who completes the journey of faith. He paid no attention to the shame of the cross. He suffered there because of the joy he was looking forward to. Then he sat down at the right hand of the throne of God.* [Hebrews 12:1-2]

Reader 2: Victoria did some things that she couldn't forgive herself for. Some of these are well-known to her family and her support group. Some she thought she would take to her grave, never sharing with another person.

When the temptation to use came upon her, she sometimes reminded herself of these things. Her guilt and shame motivated her to stay sober. Soon the urge to use would fade away.

After discussing the verses above with a Christian friend, Victoria realized there was something lacking in her strategy. Sure. She avoided using. But she came to realize that forcing herself to behave out of fear and shame was not a very joy-filled way to live.

Victoria longed to be like Jesus, who was motivated by joy. Jesus endured the difficulty of the cross by thinking about the joy set before him—the joy of returning in glory to His Father's right hand and the joy of saving and redeeming lost people. In fact, he despised the shame—treating it like it was an enemy.

Victoria wanted to be motivated by joy, not guilt and shame.

Facilitator Questions

Are you motivated in your recovery by joy or by shame and guilt?

_____
_____
_____

Do guilt and shame help or hurt your recovery?

_____
_____
_____

Reader 3: We've confessed our sins to God and to each other. We've confessed that we attempted to motivate ourselves with guilt and shame. Let's continue that confession in personal, silent prayer.

Reader 4: (Announcement of forgiveness, grace, and mercy) Jesus was able to endure the agony of the cross because he expected joy at the end of his suffering. When people lied about him, he thought about the joy that would follow. When the authorities conspired to have him arrested on false charges, he thought about the joy that would follow. When the Roman justice system unfairly sentenced him to death, he thought about the joy that would follow. When people mocked him, when they beat him, when they lined the street to stare at him as he dragged a cross to the hill where he would die, he thought about the joy that would follow.

Jesus knew there would be joy when his name was cleared. He would return to the Father as a champion. He also knew that all of Heaven would rejoice that the sins of the world were paid for.

Because our sins are paid for, we also will enter Heaven with joy.

10 God always gives you all the grace you need. So you will only have to suffer for a little while. Then God himself will build you up again. He will make you strong and steady. And he has chosen you to share in his eternal glory because you belong to Christ. [1 Peter 5:10]

Because of Jesus' life and work, we are given all the grace we need. Our guilt and embarrassment will be washed away. Even now, we can experience the freedom of forgiveness and we can look forward to the joy of Heaven. Therefore, I forgive you all your sins in the name of the Father and of the Son and of the Holy Spirit.

Everyone: Amen.

Facilitator Questions

What is a joy you are looking forward to in your recovery?

_____
_____
_____

Instead of guilt and shame, how can joy motivate you?

_____
_____
_____

HOW TO GROW

Reader 1: (Scripture) *²⁴ What I'm about to tell you is true. Unless a grain of wheat falls to the ground and dies, it remains only one seed. But if it dies, it produces many seeds. ²⁵ Anyone who loves their life will lose it. But anyone who hates their life in this world will keep it and have eternal life. [John 12:24-25]*

Reader 2: Jimmy was in treatment because he needed a break from the problems drugs and alcohol had caused him. But, he also missed certain friends, certain places, and certain things he used to do. He didn't want to give them up completely. He secretly wished there was a way he could hold on to them. He also wished there was a way he could still get intoxicated once in a while. Nothing crazy—just a can here and there, or some drugs on special occasions. But giving it up completely didn't seem realistic.

Jimmy wasn't ready to put his old life to death by stopping drug and alcohol use entirely. And he didn't like the idea of being a goody-two-shoes, a schoolboy, or clean-cut. That wasn't him.

What Jimmy didn't know was that any love or affection for his old life would cause him to lose his sobriety. If sobriety was going to stick, he needed to build a new life and put his old life to death.

Facilitator Questions

Do you love or hate the life you had in addiction?

_____

_____

_____

To stay sober, what parts of your old life do you still need to put to death?

_____

_____

_____

Reader 3: We have confessed our sins to God and to each other. We have confessed that we still love aspects of our old life in addiction. We have also confessed that there are parts of our old life that we have yet to put to death. Let's take a moment to continue our confession in personal, silent prayer.

Reader 4: (Announcement of forgiveness, grace, and mercy) Jesus' death and resurrection can be compared to the life of a plant. Jesus's earthly body was a seed that died and was buried in the ground. When he entered the grave, he took our sin, our shame, and our embarrassment with him. When he rose from the dead, we rose with him into new life.

> *20 I have been crucified with Christ. I don't live any longer, but Christ lives in me. Now I live my life in my body by faith in the Son of God. He loved me and gave himself for me. [Galatians 2:20]*

> *And*

> *5 By being baptized, we have been joined with him in a death like his. So we will certainly also be joined with him in a resurrection like his. 6 We know that what we used to be was nailed to the cross with him. That happened so our bodies that were ruled by sin would lose their power. So we are no longer slaves of sin. 7 That's because those who have died have been set free from sin. [Romans 6:5-7]*

Our old lives—all our sins, all our mistakes, all our bad choices—are dead in Christ. They are buried in the grave and they will stay there. We now have new life in Christ. We are no longer slaves to sin. We are free. Therefore, I forgive you all your sins in the name of the Father and of the Son and of the Holy Spirit.

Everyone: Amen.

Facilitator Questions:

What do you want to do with the new life you have been given?

_____

_____

_____

Are there some things you are glad are dead about your old life—things you won't miss and don't want to experience again?

_____

_____

_____

HOW TO FOCUS

Reader 1: (Scripture) *No servant can serve two masters; for either he will hate the one and love the other, or else he will be devoted to one and despise the other. You cannot serve God and wealth."* [Matthew 6:24]

Be alert and of sober mind. Your enemy the devil prowls around like a roaring lion looking for someone to devour. [1 Peter 5:8]

Reader 2: Samantha used to serve her addiction. Everything she said and did was meant to help her get high or drunk. Her whole mind was focused on her god: Drugs and Alcohol.

Later when she entered treatment, she sometimes felt like she served two masters—addiction and sobriety. She hated what drugs and alcohol had done to her life, but she also wished she could still get high or drunk.

Now that she has 3 years of sobriety under her belt, she is serving one master again. This time she is single-minded about staying sober. She knows that she can't serve God and Addiction. And even though she has no desire to go back to her old life, she stays focused on sobriety because she knows that Addiction is a lion, waiting to devour her again.

Facilitator Questions

Are you single-minded, or are you double-minded about your sobriety?

_____

_____

_____

Why is it important for you to be single-minded about sobriety?

_____

_____

_____

Reader 3: We have confessed our sins to God and to each other. We've confessed that we are not always single-minded about our sobriety. We've also confessed the reasons it is important for us to stay sober. Let's take a moment to continue our confession in personal, silent prayer.

Reader 4: (Announcement of forgiveness, grace, and mercy) While he was still on earth, Jesus prayed this prayer to the father. It was a prayer on behalf of the disciples and on behalf of you and me.

> [20] *"I do not pray only for them. I pray also for everyone who will believe in me because of their message. [21] Father, I pray they will be one, just as you are in me and I am in you. I want them also to be in us. Then the world will believe that you have sent me. [22] I have given them the glory you gave me. I did this so they would be one, just as we are one. [23] I will be in them, just as you are in me. This is so that they may be brought together perfectly as one. Then the world will know that you sent me. It will also show the world that you have loved those you gave me, just as you have loved me. [John 17:20-23]*

Jesus prays we would have unity with him and with the Father. Our unity with Jesus and the Father is the peak of single-mindedness. If we are unified with them, we do not desire drugs and alcohol. In order to make this unity possible, Jesus took away our guilt and brokenness. He purifies us so we can be one with each other and with God. Therefore, I forgive you all your sins in the name of the Father and of the Son and of the Holy Spirit.

Everyone: Amen.

Facilitator Questions

What would your life be like if you were single-minded and sober for the next 3-5 years?

_____
_____
_____

How do you think someone would think and act if they were at one with Jesus and the Father?

_____
_____
_____

WIN AT THE SOBRIETY RACE

Reader 1: (Scripture) [24] *In a race all the runners run. But only one gets the prize. You know that, don't you? So run in a way that will get you the prize.* [25] *All who take part in the games train hard. They do it to get a crown that will not last. But we do it to get a crown that will last forever.* [26] *So I do not run like someone who doesn't run toward the finish line. I do not fight like a boxer who hits nothing but air.* [27] *No, I train my body and bring it under control. Then after I have preached to others, I myself will not break the rules. If I did break them, I would fail to win the prize.*
[1 Corinthians 9:24-27]

Reader 2: John wants to get sober, but he's not sure if he can. He has checked himself into rehab and he is grateful for the support and structure. But he knows that it can't last forever. At some point, he has to leave the rehab. Then what?

John is a little worried that he won't stay sober when leaves. But he's not worried enough to begin training for it. He is a bit like a marathon runner who shows up on race day with a positive attitude, but not much else. For John to finish the race, he needs to discipline himself and train.

Good runners use good self-control to win races. They don't stay up late, they avoid worthless junk food, and they may even miss out on entertainment and nights out. Good runners also train for endurance. They run, sprint, lift weights, and stretch.

Unfortunately, John left rehab unprepared and soon got into trouble with drugs and alcohol again.

Facilitator Questions

Is staying sober worthwhile to pursue?

_____

_____

_____

Are you training for sobriety as hard as you should?

_____

_____

_____

Reader 3: We've confessed our sins to God and to each other. We've shared why sobriety is worth pursuing. And we've shared that we need to train harder. Let's take a moment to continue our confession in personal, silent prayer.

Reader 4: (Announcement of forgiveness, grace, and mercy) Jesus ran the race of life like no one else. He endured trouble no one else could bear. He gained a victory no one else qualified for. Jesus sees our lack of athleticism and has mercy on us. He makes it possible for us to win the race. First, he accepts every fine and penalty we deserve for our mistakes in the race of life. We are forgiven and set free from all our mistakes and sins. Then he breathes life into lungs that lack oxygen, he builds up muscles that had atrophied, and he restores a beating heart to a body that had collapsed in sin. Now when we face any troubles or hardships in our life, we can think of it as pure joy, knowing that it is not punishment, but training designed to make us victorious.

> [2] *My brothers and sisters, you will face all kinds of trouble. When you do, think of it as pure joy.* [3] *Your faith will be tested. You know that when this happens it will produce in you the strength to continue.* [4] *And you must allow this strength to finish its work. Then you will be all you should be. You will have everything you need. [James 1:2-4]*

Therefore, I forgive you all your sins, and I encourage you to run toward victory, in the name of the Father and of the Son, and of the Holy Spirit.

Everyone: Amen.

Facilitator Questions

Can you share an example of when God gave you the strength to continue?

_____

_____

_____

What will you be like when you become all you should be?

_____

_____

_____

WALK IN THE LIGHT

Reader 1: (Scripture) *¹⁹ Here is the judgment. Light has come into the world, but people loved darkness instead of light. They loved darkness because what they did was evil. ²⁰ Everyone who does evil deeds hates the light. They will not come into the light. They are afraid that what they do will be seen. ²¹ But anyone who lives by the truth comes into the light. They live by the truth with God's help. They come into the light so that it will be easy to see their good deeds.* [John 3:19-21]

Reader 2: When Cathy was drinking and smoking, she did a lot of wrong things that hurt a lot of people. Looking back on that time, she realized that she was walking in darkness. She did things while walking in the darkness of addiction that she would be scared or embarrassed to do in the light of sobriety. So, she stayed hidden in the darkness. She was afraid of having her past exposed. She didn't want anyone to know what she used to do.

Now that she is sober, Cathy wants to walk in the light as much as she can. She keeps herself busy with positive and uplifting activities. She resists doing anything that could make her feel ashamed afterward.

Living in the light has helped Cathy stay sober for 8 months!

Facilitator Questions

How is an addiction like walking in the darkness?

_____
_____
_____

What did walking in darkness do to you?

_____
_____
_____

Reader 3: We've confessed our sins to God and to each other. We've confessed that addiction was like walking in the darkness. And we've confessed that the darkness did bad things to us. Let's take a moment to continue our confession in personal, silent prayer.

Reader 4: (Announcement of forgiveness, grace, and mercy) No matter how dark the darkness we have walked in, we are forgiven. Jesus shines in the darkness and gives us hope. His light overcomes darkness. Those who follow him will no longer walk in darkness because they have been given the gift of light.

The people who are now living in darkness
have seen a great light.
They are now living in a very dark land. But
a light has shined on them. [Isaiah 9:2]

And

[5] The light shines in the darkness. But the darkness has not overcome the light. [John 1:5]

And

"I am the light of the world. Anyone who follows me will never walk in darkness. They will
have that light. They will have life." [John 8:12]

Therefore, because of Jesus' power over darkness, I forgive you all your sins and encourage you to step out of the dark and into the light, in the name of the Father and of the Son, and of the Holy Spirit.

Everyone: Amen.

Facilitator Questions

In what ways is Jesus a light to you?

_____

_____

_____

What does it mean to walk in the light?

_____

_____

_____

RATE YOURSELF

Reader 1: (Scripture)
So here is what I say to every one of you. Don't think of yourself more highly than you should. Be reasonable when you think about yourself. Keep in mind the faith God has given to each of you. [Romans 12:3]

Reader 2: This is not Daniel's first rodeo. He has been in and out of treatment so many times that his behavioral health chart now has the words "chronic relapser" written in it. Daniel has relapsed for reasonable reasons, and he has relapsed for no reason at all.

"I was in the store, and I just bought a bottle," is what he said during intake at his latest rehab.

The intake worker asked him, "what do you think your chances are this time around?" Daniel thought about it and said, "it's probably 50/50."

The intake worker wrote this on the paperwork: "Daniel voices a desire to quit. But, he is unable to describe what is different about this round of treatment. This makes him at high risk for relapse."

Facilitator Questions

Thinking about your whole life, how do rate your progress up to this point? Are you better than you were, worse, or no change?

_____

_____

_____

How do rate your risk of relapse?

_____

_____

_____

Reader 3: We've confessed our sins to God and each other. We've admitted our progress isn't perfect and that we are at risk for relapse. Let's take a moment to continue our confession in personal, silent prayer.

Reader 4: (Announcement of forgiveness, grace, and mercy) God does not judge us based on our relapses. He loves us whether we succeed or fail at staying sober. The Bible says

[13] No one has greater love than the one who gives their life for their friends. [John 15:13]

And

[6] At just the right time Christ died for ungodly people. He died for us when we had no power of our own. [7] It is unusual for anyone to die for a godly person. Maybe someone would be willing to die for a good person. [8] But here is how God has shown his love for us. While we were still sinners, Christ died for us. [Romans 5:6-8

Jesus' love for you began before you got sober, and it won't end if you relapse. Martin Luther says something that applies here:

"So, when the devil throws your sins in your face and declares that you deserve death and hell, tell him this: "I admit that I deserve death and hell, what of it? For I know One who suffered and made satisfaction on my behalf. His name is Jesus Christ, Son of God, and where He is, there I shall be also!"

Therefore, I assure you that regardless of your record, God rates you favorably. I forgive you all your sins in the name of the Father and of the Son, and of the Holy Spirit.

Everyone: Amen.

Facilitator Questions

What would you tell a friend who said this about him or herself, "When God sees me coming, he rolls his eyes and says, 'not this knucklehead again?'"

_____

_____

_____

Does knowing that you are forgiven before you ever relapse make it easier or harder to stay sober?

_____

_____

_____

CONTROL YOUR ANGER

Reader 1: (Scripture) *27 "But here is what I tell you who are listening. Love your enemies. Do good to those who hate you. 28 Bless those who call down curses on you. And pray for those who treat you badly. 29 Suppose someone slaps you on one cheek. Let them slap you on the other cheek as well. Suppose someone takes your coat. Don't stop them from taking your shirt as well. 30 Give to everyone who asks you. And if anyone takes what belongs to you, don't ask to get it back. 31 Do to others as you want them to do to you.* [Luke 6:27-28]

Reader 2: Jerome didn't want to use drugs or alcohol again. But when he got angry, he was at risk for relapse.

Treatment providers, probation officers, and even friends and family could really tick him off. Sometimes he got overwhelmed with things in his life. It was then he wanted to give up and go out to get wasted. He didn't forget the consequences of using. But in the moment of anger, he stopped caring about the consequences: "To Hell with it all! I'm getting drunk today!"

For him to stay sober, he needed to find a way to calm down and control his anger. But praying for his enemies, doing good deeds to those that hate him? If he followed that advice, who knows what kind of terrible things could happen to him. He worried that he would be defenseless and that people would take advantage of him.

Facilitator Questions

Do anger or frustration cause you to want to use?

_____

_____

_____

Did you have conflicts with people over your drinking or drug use?

_____

_____

_____

Reader 3: We've confessed our sins to God and each other. We've admitted that our anger gets out of control and makes us want to use. We've also confessed there were times we had more conflicts because of our addiction. Let's continue that confession in personal, silent prayer.

Reader 4: (Announcement of forgiveness, grace, and mercy) God loves his enemies. He does good things—even to people who hate him. He causes the sun to shine down on his enemies and causes the rain to water their crops. Even when the people of earth refuse to acknowledge him and his love, he blesses them with many wondrous gifts. And when his enemies attempted to kill him, he did not turn on them in anger. Instead, he prayed for them.

> *3 The soldiers brought them to the place called the Skull. There they nailed Jesus to the cross. He hung between the two criminals. One was on his right and one was on his left. 34 Jesus said, "Father, forgive them. They don't know what they are doing." [Luke 23:34]*

When we sin, God is slow to become angry at us.

> *15 But Lord, you are a God who is tender and kind.*
> *You are gracious.*
> *You are slow to get angry.*
> *You are faithful and full of love. [Psalm 86:15]*

God doesn't wait to love us until we have made ourselves deserving of his love. He loves us first.

> *10 Here is what love is. It is not that we loved God. It is that he loved us and sent his Son to give his life to pay for our sins. [1 John 4:10]*

Therefore, I assure you that God loves you and wants a good relationship with you. I forgive you all your sins in the name of the Father and of the Son, and of the Holy Spirit.

Everyone: Amen.

Facilitator Questions

What are some ways God shows his love to you?

_____
_____
_____

What are some ways you can control your anger and avoid relapse?

_____
_____
_____

REST IN GOD'S LOVE

Reader 1: (Scripture) *⁴ Love is patient. Love is kind. It does not want what belongs to others. It does not brag. It is not proud. ⁵ It does not dishonor other people. It does not look out for its own interests. It does not easily become angry. It does not keep track of other people's wrongs.*

⁶ Love is not happy with evil. But it is full of joy when the truth is spoken. ⁷ It always protects. It always trusts. It always hopes. It never gives up.⁸ Love never fails. [1 Corinthians 13:4-8]

Reader 2: When Angel got clean and sober, he had to face a lot of things about himself that he preferred to avoid. There were images in his mind of things he had done--haunting images. There were memories of promises he did not keep, opportunities he let go, responsibilities he had ignored, and the people he had let down. It hurt him to think about these things. He felt embarrassed.

In a Bible study, Angel heard 1 Corinthians 13 and realized how unloving he had been while he was using. He wasn't patient or kind. He took things that belonged to others. He bragged and was proud. He dishonored other people through his words and actions. He only cared about his own interests. He quickly got angry. He was resentful—keeping track of other people's wrongs. He was happy to do things that he would now call wrong or evil. He was upset when people told the truth to him. He failed to protect others. He was untrustworthy and trusted no one. He was hopeless. He had given up.

Facilitator Questions

Were you a loving person when you were using?

_____

_____

_____

Did your drug of choice treat you in a loving way?

_____

_____

_____

Reader 3: We have confessed our sins to God and each other. We've shared ways were not loving to others. We have also discussed how unloving our drug of choice was to us. Let's continue that confession in personal, silent prayer.

Reader 4: (Announcement of forgiveness, grace, and mercy) God is love. God is patient with you. God is kind. He does not want to take from you. He doesn't brag or put you down. He is not proud. He does not dishonor you or treat you as worthless. God does not look out for his own interests—he sacrifices to give you good gifts. God does not easily become angry. He does not keep track of the wrongs you have done. He doesn't throw them in your face. God is not happy when evil is done; he is saddened when he sees sin and wrongdoing. But he is full of joy when the truth is spoken. God always protects. God always trusts. God always hopes. God never gives up. God never fails.

> *9 Here is how God showed his love among us. He sent his one and only Son into the world. He sent him so we could receive life through him. [1 John 4:9]*

God will forgive anything you have done, and he loves you. Therefore, I forgive you all your sins in the name of the Father and of the Son, and of the Holy Spirit.

Everyone: Amen.

Facilitator Questions

Pick one of the descriptions of God's love and share why it is meaningful to you.

_____

_____

_____

Who has treated you with love?

_____

_____

_____

FOCUS ON THE GOOD

Reader 1: (Scripture) *⁸ Finally, my brothers and sisters, always think about what is true. Think about what is noble, right and pure. Think about what is lovely and worthy of respect. If anything is excellent or worthy of praise, think about those kinds of things. [Philippians 4:8]*

Reader 2: Paul often thought about drinking and drug use. Sometimes these thoughts became almost an obsession. Maybe he thought about drinking and smoking so much because when Paul drank, he felt happy. And he enjoyed spreading his happiness to others. There was often laughter, joking, and a sense of brotherhood as he passed his bottle around.

The problem was when the money ran out, the good times stopped. The laughter, the joking, and the sense of brotherhood were gone. His happiness turned into a hangover.

Paul wondered if there was a better way. Could he experience happiness and joy without a hangover? Could he spread lasting and healthy happiness to others?

Facilitator Questions

Are drinking and drug use excellent and praiseworthy activities that you want to promote?

_____
_____
_____

Did drinking and drug use cause you to like and promote things that shouldn't be promoted?

_____
_____
_____

Reader 3: We have confessed our sins to God and each other. We've confessed that drinking and drug use were not good things to promote or participate in. We've also confessed that drinking and drug use caused us to like and promote things that were not good. Let's continue that confession in personal, silent prayer.

Reader 4: (Announcement of forgiveness, grace, and mercy) Jesus focused on the good. He did what was noble, pure, lovely, admirable, excellent, and praiseworthy. He did not chase superficial or negative activities. Instead, he chose to focus on the incredibly meaningful mission of saving humankind—even when that meant being humbled and killed.

⁵ As you deal with one another, you should think and act as Jesus did.

⁶ In his very nature he was God.
Jesus was equal with God. But Jesus didn't take advantage of that fact.

⁷ Instead, he made himself nothing.
He did this by taking on the nature of a servant.
He was made just like human beings.

⁸ He appeared as a man.
He was humble and obeyed God completely.
He did this even though it led to his death.
Even worse, he died on a cross! [Philippians 2:5-8]

Jesus knows that we have focused on worthless things—and on things that were no good at all. So, in his mercy, he lived the life we could not. He became a humble servant and died on the cross so that he could take away our guilt and shame. Therefore, I forgive you all your sins in the name of the Father and of the Son, and of the Holy Spirit.

Everyone: Amen.

Facilitator Questions

Do you have an important mission in this life that gives you a reason to stay sober?

_____
_____
_____

What kinds of excellent and praiseworthy things do you want to focus on this week?

_____
_____
_____

OVERCOME SELF-PITY

Reader 1: (Scripture)

> [7] I can't sleep. I've become
> like a bird alone on a roof.
>
> [8] All day long my enemies laugh at me.
> Those who make fun of me use my name as a curse.
>
> [9] I eat ashes as my food.
> My tears fall into what I'm drinking.
>
> [10] You were very angry with me.
> So you picked me up and threw me away.
>
> [11] The days of my life are like an evening shadow.
> I dry up like grass. [Psalm 102:7-11]

Reader 2: Eli can't believe how bad things have gotten. He is living on the street. He feels physically sick. And he hasn't had a good night's sleep in days.

He was beaten up and robbed over a few dollars last week. His family and friends chase him off when he tries to see them. Eli is mad at all the fake people in his life. And he is sick of all the negativity.

In his misery, Eli blames circumstances and other people for his situation. He also forgets that many other people are in similar or worse situations. So, he has no compassion for anyone but himself.

In a pit of self-pity and bitterness, he decides to forget about everything that is bothering him and just get drunk.

Facilitator Questions

Do you engage in self-pity?

_____

_____

_____

Have you drunk alcohol or used drugs because of self-pity?

_____

_____

_____

Reader 3: We've confessed our sins to God and each other. We've confessed that we have engaged in self-pity and that we drank and used drugs because of self-pity. Let's continue that confession in personal, silent prayer.

Reader 4: (Announcement of forgiveness, grace, and mercy) Even though Jesus felt real pain and experienced true injustice, he never engaged in self-pity. And that is good news for us. Why? Because if Jesus had stooped to self-pity, he never would have died for our sins.

Instead of self-pity, Jesus put our suffering first, and his own suffering second.

Peter says this about Jesus.

> [23] *People shouted at him and made fun of him. But he didn't do the same thing back to them. When he suffered, he didn't say he would make them suffer. Instead, he trusted in the God who judges fairly. [1 Peter 2:23]*

When Jesus trusted in God, he was able to face rejection, humiliation, and public failure without resorting to sinful self-pity or bitterness. His perfect trust in God allowed him to go through with the crucifixion, knowing that no matter what happened here on earth, God would judge fairly. A mere human could never have trusted God enough to endure the pain and injustice of the crucifixion. A mere human would have shouted back in anger and made fun of his "haters." A mere human would make others suffer for what they had done.

But not Jesus. Because of his trust in God and his divine compassion for us, we who engage in self-pity can be saved. Because of his quickness to forgive and love, we who are bitter and unloving will be accepted into heaven. Therefore, I forgive you all your sins in the name of the Father and of the Son, and of the Holy Spirit.

Everyone: Amen.

Facilitator Questions

How can you snap out of self-pity?

_____
_____
_____

How would your life be different if you had Jesus' trust in God and his compassion for others?

_____
_____
_____

OVERCOME BOREDOM

Reader 1: (Scripture) [24] *A person can't do anything better than eat, drink and be satisfied with their work. I'm finally seeing that those things also come from the hand of God.* [25] *Without his help, who can eat or find pleasure?* [Ecclesiastes 2:24-25]

> [6] *You gain a lot when you live a godly life. But you must be happy with what you have.* [7] *We didn't bring anything into the world. We can't take anything out of it.* [8] *If we have food and clothing, we will be happy with that.* [1 Timothy 6:6-8]

Reader 2: Neil got SO bored he could hardly stand it. Boredom became a torture that he longed to be released from. In the agony of boredom, his mind would turn to alcohol, weed. . . anything that could cancel out his boredom.

It was hard for Neil to be happy with simple things like a good meal, an ordinary day, or doing a chore that was productive and helpful. He wanted more than these things. He craved celebrations and thrilling adventures. Sometimes he longed for the excitement of the old days when his drinking and drug use seemed rowdy and fun.

But after a while even drinking and drugging became boring. He drank and used drugs just to feel normal. And when he wasn't high or drunk, he was miserable and unhappy.

Facilitator Questions

Has boredom ever prompted you to drink or use drugs?

_____
_____
_____

Did you ever drink or use drugs because you wanted more excitement and fun?

_____
_____
_____

Reader 3: We've confessed our sins to God and to each other. We've shared that boredom or the desire for excitement prompted us to drink and use drugs. Let's continue our confession in personal, silent prayer.

Reader 4: (Announcement of forgiveness, grace, and mercy) The Bible doesn't tell us if Jesus ever felt bored. However, we do know that Jesus didn't demand entertainment and thrills. He simply worked hard to help others.

> *23 Jesus went all over Galilee. There he taught in the synagogues. He preached the good news of God's kingdom. He healed every illness and sickness the people had. 24 News about him spread all over Syria. People brought to him all who were ill with different kinds of sicknesses. Some were suffering great pain. Others were controlled by demons. Some were shaking wildly. Others couldn't move at all. And Jesus healed all of them. 25 Large crowds followed him. People came from Galilee, from the area known as the Ten Cities, and from Jerusalem and Judea. Others came from the area across the Jordan River. [Matthew 25-4:23]*

Jesus' ministry on earth was a busy one. But his last job was the most difficult. About that job, he said from the cross, "it is finished," meaning that all the sins of the world are now forgiven, and God will never hold them against us. Therefore, I forgive you all your sins in the name of the Father, and of the Son, and of the Holy Spirit.

Everyone: Amen.

Facilitator Questions

How can you overcome boredom?

_____

_____

_____

What kind of work can you find enjoyment in?

_____

_____

_____

HOW TO BE STRONG

Reader 1: (Scripture) *So I wouldn't become proud of myself, I was given a problem. This problem caused pain in my body. It is a messenger from Satan to make me suffer. ⁸ Three times I begged the Lord to take it away from me. ⁹ But he said to me, "My grace is all you need. My power is strongest when you are weak." So I am very happy to brag about how weak I am. Then Christ's power can rest on me. ¹⁰ Because of how I suffered for Christ, I'm glad that I am weak. I am glad in hard times. I am glad when people say mean things about me. I am glad when things are difficult. And I am glad when people make me suffer. When I am weak, I am strong. [2 Corinthians 12:7-8]*

Reader 2: Reggie hated his relapses. Each time he relapsed, the devil would fill Reggie's mind with cruel and negative thoughts.

> *You screwed up again, dummy. You let everybody down, you loser. Everyone knows what you did. You're disgusting. You don't deserve any more chances.*

After a relapse, Reggie wished the relapse had never happened. Reggie begged God to help him. But he didn't want God to work through his weakness. Instead, he wished that he could be strong. He wanted to be the kind of person who didn't mess up and who never needed help.

Unfortunately, the desire to be strong and to do things on his own—without God's help—led to continued relapses.

Facilitator Questions

After a relapse, or when hungover, did you say cruel and negative things about yourself?

_____

_____

_____

Did you fail when you tried to be strong and fix things on your own?

_____

_____

_____

Reader 3: We've confessed our sins to God and to each other. We admitted that we said cruel and negative things about ourselves. We also confessed that we failed when we tried to be strong and fix things on our own. Let's take a moment to continue that confession in personal, silent prayer.

Reader 4: (Announcement of forgiveness, grace, and mercy) We do not need to be strong for God to love us and accept us. We are not disqualified from serving God because of our weaknesses, past decisions, or inability to fix ourselves.

In fact, there is nothing that can separate us from his love for us.

> [37] *No! In all these things we are more than winners! We owe it all to Christ, who has loved us.* [38] *I am absolutely sure that not even death or life can separate us from God's love. Not even angels or demons, the present or the future, or any powers can separate us.* [39] *Not even the highest places or the lowest, or anything else in all creation can separate us. Nothing at all can ever separate us from God's love. That's because of what Christ Jesus our Lord has done. [Romans 8:37-39]*

When we lose confidence in ourselves and our power, God says, "You can put your confidence in me." When we feel weak, God says, "let me be your strength." When we are crushed by our relapses, he promises, I will remove the weight of your sins." Nothing can separate us from the love of God. Therefore, I forgive you all your sins in the name of the Father, and of the Son, and of the Holy Spirit.

Everyone: Amen.

Facilitator Questions

How could your weakness be a good thing?

_____

_____

_____

Have you ever experienced success that came from the grace of God, not from anything you did?

_____

_____

_____

STOP CHASING THINGS

Reader 1: *(Scripture)*

³¹ So don't worry. Don't say, 'What will we eat?' Or, 'What will we drink?' Or, 'What will we wear?' ³² People who are ungodly run after all those things. Your Father who is in heaven knows that you need them. ³³ But put God's kingdom first. Do what he wants you to do. Then all those things will also be given to you. ³⁴ So don't worry about tomorrow. Tomorrow will worry about itself. Each day has enough trouble of its own. [Matthew 6:31-34]

Self-Examination: Meditation LAW

Reader 2: Jim worried about stuff all the time. When he worried, he looked to drugs and alcohol to fix the things he worried about. For example, he worried about feeling depressed. So, he would ask himself, "What shall I do to feel better?" When he was anxious or upset, he wondered, "How can I relax and calm down?" When he was bored, he wondered, "Where can I get some excitement?" When he was lonely, he wondered, "Where can I find companionship?" No matter the question, the answer always seemed to be drugs and alcohol.

Jim could have taken things one day at a time and put his trust in God to provide what he needed. He could have put the Kingdom of God first. He could have focused on what God wanted him to do.

Instead, Jim ran to alcohol and drugs to feel better, to relax and calm down, to get some excitement, and to find companionship.

Facilitator Questions

What do you worry about?

_____

_____

_____

Have you run to alcohol for what you worried you needed?

_____

_____

_____

Reader 3: We have confessed our sins to God and to each other. We've admitted we ran to alcohol and drugs for things we worried about. We've also shared some of our worries. Let's take a moment to continue that confession in personal, silent prayer.

Reader 4: (Announcement of forgiveness, grace, and mercy) God understands that we need things. He doesn't withhold anything from us.

> *31 What should we say then? Since God is on our side, who can be against us? 32 God did not spare his own Son. He gave him up for us all. Then won't he also freely give us everything else? [Romans 8:31-32]*

God holds nothing back for himself, not even his own son. Because he is God, he doesn't need anything. Because he doesn't need anything himself, he has no reason to hold things back from us. Instead, he shares generously. We can be confident that he will give us everything we need. Most importantly, he gives us full and complete forgiveness in Christ. With God on our side, we have nothing—absolutely nothing—to worry about. Therefore, I forgive you all your sins in the name of the Father, and of the Son, and of the Holy Spirit.

Everyone: Amen.

Facilitator Questions

When you are worried about something, what can help you stop worrying?

_____

_____

_____

How can we put God's Kingdom first?

_____

_____

_____

DEALING WITH OUR OWN SIN

Reader 1: (Scripture)

A human heart is more dishonest than anything else.
It can't be healed.
Who can understand it? [Jeremiah 17:9]

Reader 2: Five people entered rehab and started to think about what they had done while in their addiction. They could see they had done wrong.

- **Ronny** repented and believed in God's forgiveness. He became grateful and wanted to serve God.

- **Naomi** listened to Satan who accused her and told her she couldn't be forgiven. She became hopeless.

- **Stanley** blamed other people for his problems. He became angry and defensive.

- **Abby** blamed forces outside her control, like society, the government, her environment, her genes, or her upbringing. She became resentful and easily offended.

- **Harold** never showed weakness he thought it was stupid to ask for forgiveness when he knew what he was doing. He became tough and distant.

Facilitator Questions

Did you do wrong things when you were in your addiction?

_____

_____

_____

Which response or combination of responses do you have when you realize you did wrong?

_____

_____

_____

Reader 3: We have confessed our sins to God and to each other. We've confessed that we are sinful and that we often don't respond to our sin in a God-pleasing way. Let's continue that confession in personal, silent prayer.

Reader 4: (Announcement of forgiveness, grace, and mercy) It takes humility to confess our sins. God loves those who are humble. To those willing to be humble, he promises they will be lifted.

> [11] *All those who lift themselves up will be made humble. And those who make themselves humble will be lifted up. [Luke 14:11]*

This is why it is safe to humbly confess our sins to God. We don't have to beat ourselves up over our sins like Naomi. We don't need to blame other people like Stanley. We don't need to blame forces outside our control like Abby. And we don't need to be brave like Harold.

All we need to do is humbly ask for mercy and forgiveness.

> [14] *But they make themselves humble in my sight. They pray and look to me. And they turn from their evil ways. Then I will listen to them from heaven. I will forgive their sin. And I will heal their land. After all, they are my people. [2 Chronicles 7:14]*

In all confidence and security, we can confess our sins, knowing that he is kind and faithful.

> [9] *But God is faithful and fair. If we confess our sins, he will forgive our sins. He will forgive every wrong thing we have done. He will make us pure. [1 John 1:9]*

Based on God's many promises to those who are humble and confess, I forgive you all your sins in the name of the Father, and of the Son, and of the Holy Spirit.

Everyone: Amen.

Facilitator Questions

Is it weak and manipulative to ask for forgiveness?

_____

_____

_____

Do you believe God will forgive you all of your sins?

_____

_____

_____

SHOULD WE FEAR ADDICTION?

Reader 1: (Scripture) *[27] Having respect for the Lord leads to a longer life. But the years of evil people are cut short. [Proverbs 10:27]*

> *[27] Respect for the Lord is like a fountain that gives life.*
> *It turns you away from the jaws of death. [Proverbs 14:27]*

> *[23] Having respect for the Lord leads to life.*
> *Then you will be content and free from trouble. [Proverbs 19:23]*

Reader 2: After years of drinking, Reynalda had no fear or respect for alcohol.

Even though her drinking was dangerous for her health, her family relationships, and her status with the courts, she was not afraid.

She spent time with people that were not safe. She hung out at places that were not secure or stable. She did things while drunk that were potentially harmful.

Reynalda knew people—relatives, friends, and others—who had died early from alcohol or being intoxicated.

But no matter the risks, she kept drinking. It was as if no hazard or risky situation was enough to scare her away from drinking. Despite all the dangers and warning signs, Reynalda thought she could control alcohol and drugs.

Facilitator Questions

Did you lose your natural fear and respect for what substances can do to a person?

_____

_____

_____

Did you control your drinking and drug use or was it controlling you?

_____

_____

_____

Reader 3: We've confessed our sins to God and to each other. We've confessed that we should have feared and respected drugs and alcohol because a lack of respect can ruin a life or lead to an early death. Let's take a moment to continue that confession in personal, silent prayer.

Reader 4: (Announcement of forgiveness, grace, and mercy) There is hope for those of us who have lost our natural fear and respect for substances. Belief in God changes everything.

> [24] *"What I'm about to tell you is true. Anyone who hears my word and believes him who sent me has eternal life. They will not be judged. They have crossed over from death to life. [John 5:24]*

In the verse above, Jesus says that the path to eternal life is to hear and believe. You do not need a track record of godly living. You only need to believe.

Jesus came to earth so that we would hear and believe. This is from John 1:

> [11] *He came to what was his own. But his own people did not accept him.* [12] *Some people did accept him and did believe in his name. He gave them the right to become children of God.* [13] *To be a child of God has nothing to do with human parents. Children of God are not born because of human choice or because a husband wants them to be born. They are born because of what God does. [John 1:11-13]*

God's love for us is so strong that even if we have lived unwise lives, we can be confident in his forgiveness. Through something as simple as belief, he offers more than a pardon for our sins. He makes us dearly loved children, with all the rights and privileges given to the children of the King. Therefore, I forgive you all your sins in the name of the Father, and of the Son, and of the Holy Spirit.

Everyone: Amen.

Facilitator Questions

Could believing that you are a beloved child of God help you avoid relapse?

_____

_____

_____

How can we regain our fear and respect for substances?

_____

_____

_____

CAN FORGIVENESS PREVENT RELAPSE?

Reader 1: (Scripture) *³ So watch what you do.*

"If your brother or sister sins against you, tell them they are wrong. Then if they turn away from their sins, forgive them. ⁴ Suppose they sin against you seven times in one day. And suppose they come back to you each time and say, 'I'm sorry.' You must forgive them." [Luke 17:3-4]

Reader 2: Aaron didn't like to forgive. He knew that whenever one person hurts another, they owe the person they hurt. When things are stolen, they need to be returned—with interest. When one person disrespects another—it should be repaid with more insults or physical violence. When one person breaks another person's possession, they had better fix it. Abusers need to go to jail. Snitches need to be dealt with. Liars need to be called out publicly. People who reject you or judge you for drinking and using drugs need to be cut off so they can't reject you anymore.

This is how Aaron thought: "If you are soft on other people, they'll take advantage. So, every offense deserves a payback."

Because Aaron wanted payback and justice instead of mercy and forgiveness, he was often angry and resentful. Like a pot of water on a hot stove, he was on the verge of boiling over. A single minor issue and he could explode.

His negative attitude toward others made his mood dark and pessimistic.

Facilitator Questions

When you were in active addiction, were you resentful and angry at others?

_____

_____

_____

What price do you pay when you don't forgive?

_____

_____

_____

Reader 3: We've confessed our sins to God and to each other. We've confessed that we were angry and resentful. We also confessed that we paid a price for not forgiving. Let's take a moment to continue that confession in personal, silent prayer.

Reader 4: (Announcement of forgiveness, grace, and mercy) Sins do require payment. Without the payment for sins, humans are separated from God. This fact was symbolized in the ancient temple of the Jews. A curtain separated the people from the place where sacrifices to the Lord were made. This separate place was called the "Most Holy Room." Only priests, who were ceremonially purified could go behind the curtain, into the Most Holy Room. In the Most Holy Room, they made sacrifices on behalf of the people. The priests acted as the middleman between sinful people and a holy God.

Thankfully, God accepts Jesus' sacrifice on the cross as payment for the sins of the world. The passage below explains that the blood of Jesus acts as payment, and how his body creates a new, and living way to have a close relationship with God. Jesus is both the perfect sacrifice and the perfect priest—acting as a middleman between sinful humans and a holy God. Because of Jesus, we can now enter the Most Holy Room with confidence.

> [19] *Brothers and sisters, we are not afraid to enter the Most Holy Room. We enter boldly because of the blood of Jesus.* [20] *His way is new because he lives. It has been opened for us through the curtain. I'm talking about his body.* [21] *We also have a great priest over the house of God.* [22] *So let us come near to God with a sincere heart. Let us come near boldly because of our faith. Our hearts have been sprinkled. Our minds have been cleansed from a sense of guilt. Our bodies have been washed with pure water.* [23] *Let us hold firmly to the hope we claim to have. The God who promised is faithful.* [24] *Let us consider how we can stir up one another to love. Let us help one another to do good works.* [25] *And let us not give up meeting together. Some are in the habit of doing this. Instead, let us encourage one another with words of hope. Let us do this even more as you see Christ's return approaching.* [Hebrews 10:19-25]

We have been unforgiving. But Jesus made it possible for God to truly forgive us. Therefore, I forgive you all your sins in the name of the Father, and of the Son, and of the Holy Spirit.

Everyone: Amen.

Facilitator Questions

What does it feel like to be forgiven?

_____

_____

_____

Can forgiving others help prevent relapse?

_____

_____

_____

IS YOUR BODY HOLY?

Reader 1: (Scripture) *27 So God created mankind in his own image, in the image of God he created them; male and female he created them. [Genesis 1:27]*

19 Do you not know that your bodies are temples of the Holy Spirit, who is in you, whom you have received from God? You are not your own; 20 you were bought at a price. Therefore honor God with your bodies. [1 Corinthians 6:19-20]

Reader 2: Shontel punished her body with drugs and alcohol. She didn't mean to harm herself. But, man, did she do herself some damage over the years. Her heart, liver, kidneys, and pancreas had taken a beating from alcohol. Her teeth were damaged and missing from meth, fists, and homelessness. She has scars and fractures from assaults and fights. Her body got misused by men who didn't love or respect her. Her body was the victim of 15 years of crimes.

If her body could talk, it would cry out for help and protection. It would ask for healthy food, exercise, and some pampering. It would ask to be treated with respect and dignity. And it would ask to be allowed to live a long life.

Shontel was surprised to learn she had three important reasons to respect and care for her body. First, she learned that her body was created in the image of God—and that it deserved good treatment and protection. Second, she learned that her body is the dwelling place of the Holy Spirit. Third, she learned that she was bought for a price—meaning God recovered her from Satan's grip with Jesus' blood.

Facilitator Questions

How did you treat your body when you were drinking and using drugs?

_____

_____

_____

What price has your body paid because of drugs and alcohol?

_____

_____

_____

Reader 3: We've confessed our sins to God and to each other. We've confessed that we mistreated our bodies and that our bodies have paid a price for it. Let's take a moment to continue that confession in personal, silent prayer.

Reader 4: (Announcement of forgiveness, grace, and mercy) God gave us the bodies we currently have—and they are made in his image. However, even if we don't abuse our bodies, they will eventually break down and stop working. Our current bodies are vulnerable to death and decay. But God assures us that he will give us new bodies. What will these new bodies be like?

> 35 But someone will ask, "How are the dead raised? What kind of body will they have?" 36 How foolish! What you plant doesn't come to life unless it dies. 37 When you plant something, it isn't a completely grown plant that you put in the ground. You only plant a seed. Maybe it's wheat or something else. 38 But God gives the seed a body just as he has planned. And to each kind of seed, he gives its own body. 39 Not all earthly creatures are the same. People have one kind of body. Animals have another. Birds have another kind. Fish have still another. 40 There are also heavenly bodies as well as earthly bodies. Heavenly bodies have one kind of glory. Earthly bodies have another. 41 The sun has one kind of glory. The moon has another kind. The stars have still another. And one star's glory is different from that of another star.
>
> 42 It will be like that with bodies that are raised from the dead. The body that is planted does not last forever. The body that is raised from the dead lasts forever. 43 It is planted without honor. But it is raised in glory. It is planted in weakness. But it is raised in power. 44 It is planted as an earthly body. But it is raised as a spiritual body. [1 Corinthians 15:35-40]

When God forgives us, he doesn't only put things back the way they were; he makes things better. He doesn't just forgive us and heal our bodies; he will give us new bodies that will live forever and have honor, glory, and power. The new bodies won't be like our earthly bodies—they will be spiritual bodies. Therefore, I encourage you to look forward to your new body and I forgive you all your sins in the name of the Father, and of the Son, and of the Holy Spirit.

Everyone: Amen.

Facilitator Questions

What reasons do you have for protecting and caring for your body?

_____
_____
_____

How can you take care of your body?

_____
_____
_____

WHEN HELPING HURTS.

Reader 1: (Scripture)

 [1] *Brothers and sisters, what if someone is caught in a sin? Then you who live by the Spirit should correct that person. Do it in a gentle way. But be careful. You could be tempted too.* [Galatians 6:1]

Reader 2: Cynthia had a soft heart for anyone in trouble. She liked the misfits, the underdogs, and the outcasts. If someone needed a ride, she felt terrible turning them down. If someone was sad and hurting, she never wanted to ignore them. She felt it was her duty to listen and help them in any way she could.

The idea of correcting a person felt cold and uncaring. She wanted to "be at their level." If someone asked her to do something she didn't want to do, they could manipulate her by simply saying, "you think you're better than me!" Cynthia would immediately cave in and do what the person wanted.

Cynthia couldn't let a person harvest what they planted. Instead, she wanted to save them from the consequences of their choices. She thought she was being kind by fixing things for them.

Unfortunately, her kindness was killing her. Every time she helped somebody out, she'd end up getting high or drunk with them. She lost money, time, and personal property by helping everyone else. And because she was helping people out of jams, she didn't fulfill her obligations to her family, her children, or her work.

Sadly, when she needed a hand or someone to visit her—she was mysteriously alone. None of the people she helped were willing to help her the way she helped them.

Facilitator Questions

Have people in addiction guilted you into going along with them in their mistakes?

_____

_____

_____

Did anyone ever try to help you, but ended up enabling you instead?

_____

_____

_____

Reader 3: We've confessed our sins to God and to each other. We've confessed that we have been guilted into helping people and gotten caught up in their mistakes. We've also been enabled by others. Let's continue that confession in personal, silent prayer.

Reader 4: (Announcement of forgiveness, grace, and mercy) Sometimes it is hard to know where helping ends and sinning begins. We might make the wrong choice about helping others. People may call us out or say we think we are too good for them. Only God is right in every decision. If we have sinned by being too helpful or not helpful enough, we can find comfort in this passage. In it, God tells the descendants of Jacob (which includes us), that he has called us, we do not need to fear, and our enemies will be reduced to "nothing."

> ⁹ I took you from the ends of the earth,
> from its farthest corners I called you.
> I said, 'You are my servant';
> I have chosen you and have not rejected you.
>
> ¹⁰ So do not fear, for I am with you;
> do not be dismayed, for I am your God.
> I will strengthen you and help you;
> I will uphold you with my righteous right hand.
>
> ¹¹ "All who rage against you
> will surely be ashamed and disgraced; those
> who oppose you
> will be as nothing and perish. [Isaiah 41:9-11]

He has called us to be his servants and we can help others. We can also decide not to help if helping would harm our sobriety or contribute to another's addiction. He is with us and will strengthen us. He will uphold us with his righteous right hand. If people gossip about us or oppose us, he will deal with them. Their criticism will be reduced to "nothing." Therefore, I encourage you to be the right kind of helpful and I forgive you all your sins in the name of the Father, and of the Son, and of the Holy Spirit.

Everyone: Amen.

Facilitator Questions

What kind of help can you safely give?

_____
_____
_____

What can you do when you can't help someone?

_____
_____
_____

WE ARE DEAD TO DRINKING

Reader 1: (Scripture) *⁸ We died with Christ. So we believe that we will also live with him. ⁹ We know that Christ was raised from the dead and will never die again. Death doesn't control him anymore. ¹⁰ When he died, he died once and for all time. He did this to break the power of sin. Now that he lives, he lives in the power of God. [Romans 6:8-10]*

Reader 2: When Bobby was using drugs or drinking, he became someone else. He acted like a clown, or he said cruel things to others. Sometimes he referred to his drunk self as "Evil Bobby."

When some family members confronted him, he realized he needed to make a clean break from the past. "Drunk Bobby" needed to die with Christ. Dying with Christ meant giving up anything connected with drinking and drug use. He needed to bury his old attitude, his old way of speaking, and his old habits and preferences.

Bobby wasn't bothered by the fact his old life needed to die. In fact, he'd noticed that he didn't really like the person he had become.

Bobby was looking forward to starting a new life that was different from his life in addiction.

Facilitator Questions

Were you a different person when you drank and used drugs?

_____

_____

_____

Were you ever embarrassed by your behavior in addiction?

_____

_____

_____

Reader 3: We've confessed our sins to God and to each other. We've confessed that were different people when we were drinking and getting high. We also confessed that we were sometimes embarrassed by our behavior. Let's continue that confession in personal, silent prayer.

Reader 4: (Announcement of forgiveness, grace, and mercy) You can live a new life. You do not need to cling to old habits and ways of thinking and acting. Becoming a whole new person might sound overwhelming—not something you could do on your own.

> *⁴ But God loves us deeply. He is full of mercy. ⁵ So he gave us new life because of what Christ has done. He gave us life even when we were dead in sin. God's grace has saved you. ⁶ God raised us up with Christ. He has seated us with him in his heavenly kingdom. That's because we belong to Christ Jesus. ⁷ He has done it to show the riches of his grace for all time to come. His grace can't be compared with anything else. He has shown it by being kind to us. He was kind to us because of what Christ Jesus has done. ⁸ God's grace has saved you because of your faith in Christ. Your salvation doesn't come from anything you do. It is God's gift. ⁹ It is not based on anything you have done. No one can brag about earning it. ¹⁰ We are God's creation. He created us to belong to Christ Jesus. Now we can do good works. Long ago God prepared these works for us to do. [Ephesians 2:4-10]*

We don't have to make ourselves new on our own. How could we? We are not God. Instead, God loves us and gives us new life as a gift. We are a new creation. And long ago he planned good new things for us to do. Therefore, I forgive you all your sins in the name of the Father, and of the son, and of the Holy Spirit.

Everyone: Amen

Facilitator Questions

Do you like the thought that the old "Addicted You" has died?

_____

_____

_____

What about your new life are you most thankful for?

_____

_____

_____

NO EXCUSES

Reader 1: (Scripture)[19] *Elijah left Mount Horeb. He saw Elisha, the son of Shaphat. Elisha was plowing in a field. He was driving the last of 12 pairs of oxen. Elijah went up to him. He threw his coat around him.* [20] *Then Elisha left his oxen. He ran after Elijah. "Let me kiss my father and mother goodbye," he said. "Then I'll come with you." […]* [21] *[…]So Elisha left him and went back. He got his two oxen and killed them. He burned the plow to cook the meat. He gave it to the people, and they ate it. Then he started to follow Elijah. He became Elijah's servant. [1 Kings 19:19-21]*

Reader 2: Elisha was farming when the prophet Elijah came to see him. Elijah called him to become a prophet of the Lord. Elisha was so serious about accepting the call to be a prophet that he burned the plow and cooked the two Oxen. This shows that he did not expect to go back to plowing anymore. He was "all in" when it came to his new calling.

Bruce was called too. He was called to sobriety by his wife, his children, his parents, the legal system, and his employer. . . they all had hopes and expectations for him. If he accepted the call, he could become a great blessing by being a husband, father, child, citizen, and worker.

Instead of accepting this calling, Bruce had a million excuses for drinking and drug use. "You made me mad!" "Why are you checking up on me?" "I don't need you looking over my shoulder all the time." "I'm just going to the store." "I want to see how my friend is doing."

Facilitator Questions

What excuses have you used for drinking and getting high?

_____

_____

_____

Have you missed out on a call to responsibility or neglected an opportunity because of drinking and drugs?

_____

_____

_____

Reader 3: We have confessed our sins to God and to each other. We've confessed that we used excuses for drinking and getting high. We've also confessed that we have missed out on a call to responsibility and neglected opportunities. Let's continue that confession in personal, silent prayer.

Reader 4: (Announcement of forgiveness, grace, and mercy) Jesus never made excuses to get out of doing what his father called him to do. For example, he restored sight to a blind man on the official day of rest, even though it made the authorities mad. Jesus said he would do what God called him to do, no matter what.

"4. . .While it is still day, we must do the works of the one who sent me. Night is coming. Then no one can work. 5 While I am in the world, I am the light of the world." [John 9:4-5]

Jesus made no excuses. Jesus stuck with his calling even when he was beaten, mocked, falsely accused, and sentenced to death. It would have been understandable for Jesus to say, "Look how these people are treating me! I am not going to help them!" Instead, he allowed himself zero excuses even when it meant he would die a terrible death. The night did come for Jesus. On the cross, the sky became dark, and he received the punishment for our sins. Jesus became the sacrifice to pay for all the times we have made excuses. He was called to release us from the sentence of death we deserve for neglecting our calling. Therefore, I forgive you all your sins in the name of the Father, and of the Son, and of the Holy Spirit.

Everyone: Amen.

Facilitator Questions

Do you have a call or an opportunity now?

_____

_____

_____

What steps are you taking to fulfill your call or opportunity?

_____

_____

_____

REBELLIOUS NO MORE

Reader 1: (Scripture) *³ Like a good soldier of Christ Jesus, join with me in suffering. ⁴ A soldier does not take part in things that don't have anything to do with the army. Instead, he tries to please his commanding officer. ⁵ It is the same for anyone who takes part in a sport. They don't receive the winner's crown unless they play by the rules. ⁶ The farmer who works hard should be the first to receive a share of the crops. ⁷ Think about what I'm saying. The Lord will help you understand what all of it means. [2 Timothy 2:3-7]*

Reader 2: In the passage above, Paul is giving advice to Timothy. Paul is an older and more experienced evangelist. Timothy is younger and less experienced. The advice that Paul gives to Timothy might be helpful to a recovering addict named Desiree.

Desiree rebelled against every authority in her life. She didn't listen to her parents or older relatives who constantly warned her to stop drinking. She was annoyed by teachers, bosses, and others in authority.

Desiree also disliked rules. She wanted to do things her own way. Desiree rebelled against the basic laws of life. The soldier, the athlete, and the farmer accept they must follow the unchanging laws of their career. They bend to rules; they don't demand that rules change to fit them. Desiree thought she was an exception. She thought things should come easy and that she shouldn't have to do things unless they were enjoyable to her.

Facilitator Questions

When you were in active addiction, were you rebellious like Desiree?

_____

_____

_____

What basic rules of life do you not want to follow?

_____

_____

_____

Reader 3: We have confessed our sins to God and to each other. We've confessed our rebellion, our dislike of rules, and our desire to make the world change to fit us. Let's continue that confession in personal, silent prayer.

Reader 4: (Announcement of forgiveness, grace, and mercy) When we think back on our rebelliousness, dislike of rules, and our desire to change the world, it is easy to get frustrated with ourselves. We might wish that we had smartened up a long time ago. Paul the Apostle felt this way, too. But listen to what he concludes about his worst behavior:

> [15] *Here is a trustworthy saying that deserves full acceptance: Christ Jesus came into the world to save sinners—of whom I am the worst.* [16] *But for that very reason I was shown mercy so that in me, the worst of sinners, Christ Jesus might display his immense patience as an example for those who would believe in him and receive eternal life.* [1 Timothy 1:15-16]

The Paul who wrote the words above is the same Paul who wrote the advice to Timothy that we read on the first page. He persecuted Christians, trying to stamp out the early church. He got Christians fired from their jobs and he took away their homes and possessions. Some say he even oversaw the killing of Christians. The memory of his rebellious behavior keeps him humble and helps show others the immense patience of Jesus. Paul was the worst of sinners, but he was forgiven by Jesus. Therefore, I forgive you all your sins in the name of the Father, and of the Son, and of the Holy Spirit.

Everyone: Amen.

Facilitator Questions

Has Jesus been patient with you?

_____

_____

_____

What advice would give a younger you or what advice would you give yourself now?

_____

_____

_____

ARE YOU CLEAN AND PURE?

Reader 1: (Scripture) *²⁷ "How terrible for you, teachers of the law and Pharisees! You pretenders! You are like tombs that are painted white. They look beautiful on the outside. But on the inside they are full of the bones of the dead. They are also full of other things that are not pure and 'clean.' ²⁸ It is the same with you. On the outside you seem to be doing what is right. But on the inside you are full of what is wrong. You pretend to be what you are not. [Matthew 23: 27-28]*

Reader 2: Andre tried to balance things out. Yeah, he did drugs. . . sold drugs, too. He swore. His jokes were dirty. Inwardly, he was full of resentment, pride, and selfishness, which caused him to get into verbal and physical fights. He was not welcome in some places because his behavior was unacceptable. He lusted after women and didn't treat them well. At the end of the day, he did a lot of things it was difficult to be proud of.

But he still saw himself as a pretty decent guy. For example, he was loyal to his friends. He was handy and would help others when he was sober. If he had something, he shared. He checked up on people that might be feeling bad. And he definitely wasn't greedy like some people he knew.

Andre was covering up the bad things with the good. He was like the old-time teachers of the law, whom Jesus called white-washed tombs. They looked clean and white on the outside, but on the inside, they were full of dead bones—things that were wrong and not pure.

Facilitator Questions

What is not clean and pure about drinking and substance use?

_____

_____

_____

In active addiction, did you try to whitewash or cover up your bad actions with good actions?

_____

_____

_____

Reader 3: We've confessed our sins to God and to each other. We've confessed that drinking and drug use were not clean and pure. And we've confessed that we tried to cover up our bad actions with good actions. Let's take a moment to continue that confession in personal, silent prayer.

Reader 4: (Announcement of forgiveness, grace, and mercy) In the past, God required his people to follow special rules to stay pure and avoid contamination. For example, he required his people to perform ceremonial washing and purification before they could approach him or his altar. He also required them to stay away from certain kinds of foods and the practices of foreigners.

God no longer requires outward purity, ritual washing, or good deeds to make us pure and clean. Instead, he loves us while we are still dirty, and he cleans us through Jesus.

8But God demonstrates his own love for us in this: While we were still sinners, Christ died for us. [Romans 5:8]

Jesus' sacrifice on the cross, removes all our sins and impurities. God sends his Holy Spirit to us to help us see that we need to be washed—and that we can't do anything to clean ourselves. Then the Holy Spirit moves us to confess our sins.

> *9 If we confess our sins, he is faithful and just and will forgive us our sins and purify us from all unrighteousness.* [1 John 1:9]

Being purified and clean, we want to hang on to the feeling. We don't want to run out and get dirty right away. Because of God's love and the cleanliness, we receive from Christ, I forgive you all your sins in the name of the Father, and of the Son, and of the Holy Spirit.

Everyone: Amen.

Facilitator Questions

Why is confessing our sins—to God or to another person—good to do?

_____

_____

_____

Now that you are clean, what will you do to stay clean?

_____

_____

_____

AN INTERNAL WAR

Reader 1: (Scripture) *²¹ Here is the law I find working in me. When I want to do good, evil is right there with me. ²² Deep inside me I find joy in God's law. ²³ But I see another law working in me. It fights against the law of my mind. It makes me a prisoner of the law of sin. That law controls me. ²⁴ What a terrible failure I am! Who will save me from this sin that brings death to my body? [Romans 7:21-24]*

Reader 2: Leonard loved alcohol and drugs. Leonard hated alcohol and drugs. His feelings about his addiction were so confusing that even he could not make sense of them.

He wanted to stay sober, but he drank and used drugs anyway. When he was thinking clearly, he loved being responsible and helpful to his family. But sometimes, he would go back to his addiction.

It was like he had two different laws or sets of rules. One set of rules told him not to drink and use drugs. The other set of rules demanded that he give in to his addiction. The two sets of rules were causing a war inside of him.

Sometimes he just wanted someone to rescue him from his addiction.

Facilitator Questions

Have you ever drunk alcohol or used drugs when you were trying not to?

_____

_____

_____

Have you ever felt so frustrated about your addiction that you just wished you could be rescued?

_____

_____

_____

Reader 3: You have meditated on the law and confessed your sins to God and to each other. We admitted we lacked control of our drinking and drug use. Let us take a moment to continue that confession in personal, silent prayer.

Reader 4: (Announcement of forgiveness, grace, and mercy) Fortunately, God is a rescuer. He doesn't get mad at people who are confused, lack control, or who struggle. He doesn't turn his back on us.

> [17] *Godly people cry out, and the Lord hears them.*
> *He saves them from all their troubles.*
>
> [18] *The Lord is close to those whose hearts have been broken.*
> *He saves those whose spirits have been crushed.* [Psalm 34:17-18]

Jesus saves people who are in trouble, and he gets close to those who feel defeated. In his earthly life, he associated with sinners, people with troubles, and those whose spirits had been crushed. Even though he should have been a celebrity because of his life, teaching, and acts of charity, he was condemned, beaten, and killed. Even though he deserved a crown of glory, he chose a crown of thorns. Instead of wealthy and powerful friends, he chose to be close to poor and troubled people. He didn't just choose us as friends, he went to the cross for people like you and me. Therefore, I forgive you all your sins in the name of the Father and of the Son and of the Holy Spirit.

Everyone: Amen.

Facilitator Questions

Did God protect or rescue you from yourself and your addiction?

_____

_____

_____

What are some good ways to prevent relapse?

_____

_____

_____

HONESTLY. I TEMPT MYSELF

Reader 1: (Scripture) *[13] When a person is tempted, they shouldn't say, "God is tempting me." God can't be tempted by evil. And he doesn't tempt anyone. [14] But each person is tempted by their own evil desires. These desires lead them on and drag them away. [15] When these desires are allowed to remain, they lead to sin. And when sin is allowed to remain and grow, it leads to death. [James 1:13-15]*

Reader 2: Janice never took responsibility for her drug use and drinking. If she bought a bottle of alcohol at the store, she'd blame the store's sales and advertising for tempting her. If there was a game on television, she'd blame the game for her drinking. If she had a bad day, that was her excuse. Of course, great days had to be celebrated with alcohol or drugs, too. So, even good days were at fault for her addiction.

When the trouble caused by drugs and alcohol became too much for Janice, she eventually took a different approach. She started to look at herself. She realized she was her own worst enemy. She needed to make changes to Janice, or she'd never get sober.

It hurt at first—like a slap in the face. But soon she started to feel some hope. She couldn't fix the world and everyone in it, but with God's help, she could change herself.

Once she realized there was hope, it became easier to admit her role in her addiction. Call it confession, call it honesty, call it whatever you want. But saying the truth about her role in her addiction gave her a chance to make the changes necessary to quit drinking and drugging for good.

Facilitator Questions.

Have you blamed situations or other people for your drinking and drug use?

_____

_____

_____

What about you needs to change for you to get and stay sober?

_____

_____

_____

Reader 3: We've confessed that we blamed situations and other people for our addiction and that there are things about us that need to change. Let's take a moment to continue our reflection in personal, silent prayer.

Reader 4: (Announcement of forgiveness, grace, and mercy) We have a hard time being honest and confessing our faults. Jesus, on the other hand, took the blame for sin that was not even his. He did this on the cross, where he accepted the blame for our sins. Because he accepted the consequences of our sins, we are released from our consequences. His work on the cross not only wiped the slate clean, but it also made us righteous in God's sight. When God looks at us, he does not see our sins. He sees Jesus' righteousness.

> *[21] Christ didn't have any sin. But God made him become sin for us. So we can be made right with God because of what Christ has done for us. [2 Corinthians 5:21]*

Because Christ took responsibility for our sins, we do not need to fear punishment. God forgives our sins and calls us from darkness to his marvelous light. Therefore, I forgive you all your sins in the name of the Father and of the Son and of the Holy Spirit.

Everyone: Amen.

Facilitator Questions

What helps you take responsibility?

_____

_____

_____

What difference does it make that we have been made right with God?

_____

_____

_____

STOP GETTING BIT

Reader 1: (Scripture)

> *31 Don't look at wine when it is red.*
> *Don't look at it when it bubbles in the cup.*
> *And don't look at it when it goes down smoothly.*
>
> *32 In the end it bites like a snake.*
> *It bites like a poisonous serpent. [Proverbs 23:31-32]*

Reader 2: Right before relapse, Bernard would fantasize about drugs and alcohol. In his fantasies, drugs and alcohol were attractive and desirable. He believed they would make him feel better. They'd be fun. They'd help him escape his troubles for a while. They wouldn't hurt him. Just a little bit would be ok. No one will ever know. This would be his last time.

He focused on the fantasy while at the same time, he downplayed the reality of what drugs and alcohol had done to him and his family.

Finally, Bernard wised up. He realized that no matter how attractive drugs and alcohol seemed before he used them, they eventually bit him like a poisonous serpent. He was tired of getting bit.

Now when he thinks about drugs and alcohol, he sees through the fantasy and into reality: alcohol and drugs are snakes—people who try to handle them will get bit sooner or later.

Facilitator Questions

Have you been tricked by unrealistic fantasies about drugs and alcohol?

_____

_____

_____

Have you been bitten by addiction?

_____

_____

_____

Reader 3: We have confessed to unrealistic fantasies about drugs and alcohol, and we've confessed that drugs and alcohol have bitten us like a poisonous serpent. Let's take a moment to continue that confession in personal, silent prayer.

Reader 4: (Announcement of forgiveness, grace, and mercy) On this side of heaven, we will still get tricked by unrealistic fantasies. But God tells us that a day is coming in which we will no longer fight temptation.

> *[25] I [the LORD] will sprinkle pure water on you. Then you will be 'clean.' I will make you completely pure and 'clean.' I will take all the statues of your gods away from you. [26] I will give you new hearts. I will give you a new spirit that is faithful to me. I will remove your stubborn hearts from you. I will give you hearts that obey me. [Ezekiel 36:25-26]*

We will no longer fight with temptation because God himself will transform us—washing us and giving us a new heart. The new heart will give us the power to overcome temptation. As Christians, we have begun to change, but we will not fully beat temptation until we reach heaven. For now, God forgives our sins and calls us from darkness to his marvelous light. Therefore, I forgive you all your sins in the name of the Father and of the Son and of the Holy Spirit.

Everyone: Amen.

Facilitator Questions

Heaven is the place where we will no longer battle temptation. Describe how you think it will be when you no longer struggle with temptation.

_____

_____

_____

What helps you beat temptation?

_____

_____

_____

DON'T FOLLOW THE CROWD

Reader 1: (Scripture)

Brothers and sisters, God has shown you his mercy. So I am asking you to offer up your bodies to him while you are still alive. Your bodies are a holy sacrifice that is pleasing to God. When you offer your bodies to God, you are worshiping him in the right way. [2] Don't live the way this world lives. Let your way of thinking be completely changed. Then you will be able to test what God wants for you. And you will agree that what he wants is right. His plan is good and pleasing and perfect. [Romans 12:1-2]

Reader 2: When Sidney was a child, he told himself he would never do drugs or drink alcohol. But things changed as he got older. He started drinking here and there and spent more and more time following the crowd. Soon, he spent so much time with the crowd, that he started to dress like the crowd, talk like the crowd, and listen to the same music as the crowd. He did what they did.

He changed. And he gave up things he used to love to do.

Sidney was so influenced by the crowd that he started lowering his standards and values. He started doing things he used to be against doing. Pretty soon, the bad things he did while drunk or high started to feel normal.

In recovery, Sidney started to learn about God's love and mercy. Now he wanted to follow God instead of following people. He realized that God made him with unique abilities and interests. Sydney wanted to develop those things.

Facilitator Questions

Did drinking or drug use change you or make you give up things you loved to do?

_____

_____

_____

Did you ever lower your standards or go against your morals because of drinking or drug use?

_____

_____

_____

Reader 3: We have confessed our sins to God and to each other. We changed and we gave up things we used to love to do because of drugs and alcohol. We also started to lower our standards and values. Let us take a moment to continue that confession in personal, silent prayer.

Reader 4: (Announcement of forgiveness, grace, and mercy) Jesus never followed the crowd. He never lowered his standards. He never compromised his morality. The crowd loved him at first, but they turned on him. When Jesus didn't give the crowd what they wanted, they demanded his death.

But Jesus did not get angry, and he did not curse those that turned on him. He knew ahead of time that he would not be popular, and he even called it "blessed" to suffer from rejection by the crowd.

^{10}*Blessed are those who suffer for doing what is right.*
   The kingdom of heaven belongs to them.

   ^{11} *"Blessed are you when people make fun of you and hurt you because of me. You are also blessed when they tell all kinds of evil lies about you because of me. ^{12} Be joyful and glad. Your reward in heaven is great. In the same way, people hurt the prophets who lived long ago. [Matthew 5:10-12]*

When we are rejected by the crowd, or they make fun of us, or they lie about us, or they try to get us to relapse, we can be joyful and glad. We will know that we are becoming like Jesus because people are treating us like him. And Jesus will not reject those who follow in his footsteps. He knows that it is difficult to be hurt by the crowd, but he promises us that we are blessed. Therefore, I forgive you all your sins in the name of the Father and of the Son and of the Holy Spirit.

Everyone: Amen

Facilitator Questions

By not drinking or using drugs, could you be a blessing to others?

_____
_____
_____

How do you think Jesus wants us to treat people who do things to try to get us to relapse?

_____
_____
_____

GRACE TO SAY, "NO"

Reader 1: (Scripture) *11 God's grace has now appeared. By his grace, God offers to save all people. 12 His grace teaches us to say no to godless ways and sinful desires. We must control ourselves. We must do what is right. We must lead godly lives in today's world. 13 That's how we should live as we wait for the blessed hope God has given us. We are waiting for Jesus Christ to appear in his glory. He is our great God and Savior. [Titus 2:11-13]*

Reader 2: Ellie became completely hopeless in her addiction. The hangovers were awful. She felt guilty and ashamed for relapsing. The morning after drinking and using drugs, she became nervous about what she might have done while blacked out. Physically, she felt sick and shaky. Mentally, she was depressed, foggy, and anxious. Spiritually, she felt gross and dirty.

Ellie felt self-loathing—an intense dislike, disgust, and hatred for herself. She felt so bad that she swore she'd never drink or use drugs again.

Ultimately, it wasn't the hangover that got Ellie sober. God's love and grace taught her how to say, "No" to drugs and alcohol. Forgiveness from God and others freed her from the shame that kept her stuck. Support and encouragement from her peers and family gave her hope that things could change.

Facilitator Questions

Did addiction cause you to feel hopeless or self-loathing?

_____

_____

_____

Did hangovers, hopelessness, or self-loathing help you get sober?

_____

_____

_____

Reader 3: We have confessed our sins to God and to each other. We admitted that our addiction caused us to feel hopelessness and self-loathing. We've also admitted that hangovers, hopelessness, and self-loathing couldn't get us sober. Let's take a moment to continue that confession in personal, silent prayer.

Reader 4: (Announcement of forgiveness, grace, and mercy) God does not loathe you. He loves you.

> [1] *See what amazing love the Father has given us! Because of it, we are called children of God. And that's what we really are! The world doesn't know us because it didn't know him.* [2] *Dear friends, now we are children of God. He still hasn't let us know what we will be. But we know that when Christ appears, we will be like him. [1 John 3:1-2]*

The love of a father is a blessing to his children. Children with an earthly father grow up with a sense of safety and security. Likewise, children who have a Father in heaven will experience even more safety and security. With that safety and security, they will grow and be healthy. God wants to be our good father. He wants to claim us, raise us, and protect us now and in eternity. Therefore, I invite you to experience God's great love and care for you and to believe when I say, "Your sins are forgiven in the name of the Father and of the Son and of the Holy Spirit."

Everyone: Amen

Facilitator Questions

How does God the Father want you to treat yourself when you make a mistake or mess something up?

_____
_____
_____

How will the safety and security that comes from your Father in Heaven help you grow into a healthy and sober person?

_____
_____
_____

BECOMING SPIRITUAL AGAIN

Reader 1: (Scripture) *⁴ The god of this world has blinded the minds of those who don't believe. They can't see the light of the good news that makes Christ's glory clear. Christ is the likeness of God. ⁵ The message we preach is not about ourselves. Our message is about Jesus Christ. We say that he is Lord. And we say that we serve you because of Jesus. ⁶ God said, "Let light shine out of darkness." He made his light shine in our hearts. His light gives us the light to know God's glory. His glory is shown in the face of Christ. [2 Corinthians 4:4-6]*

Reader 2: Tim was starting to get really isolated. As more and more of his activities focused on drugs and alcohol, he felt less and less at home around the things of God. In the past, he attended church regularly and read the Bible often. But now it seemed that his spiritual life was drying up. He felt rejected and guilty.

When Tim did anything with Christians he'd feel like a hypocrite or that he wasn't welcome.

It was as if Tim was blind to the light of the good news. He couldn't see how kind and forgiving Christ was. He couldn't see how welcome and loved he was.

Tim stayed in the darkness of drinking and drug use, in part, because he couldn't see the light and glory of Jesus and the Gospel message.

Facilitator Questions

Was your spiritual life weaker or stronger when you were drinking and using drugs?

_____
_____
_____

What were you blind to when you were drinking and using drugs?

_____
_____
_____

Reader 3: You have confessed your sins to God and to each other. We've admitted that our spiritual lives were weaker in our addiction. We've also admitted that we were blind to some things because of our drinking and drug use. Let's take a moment to continue that confession in personal, silent prayer.

Reader 4: (Announcement of forgiveness, grace, and mercy) God wants us to have a full spiritual life. He knows that we have been separated from him by our own blindness and sin. So, Jesus came into our world to bring light, and life--and to help us see God's glory. In the passage below, Jesus is called the *Word*.

> *¹ In the beginning, the Word was already there. The Word was with God, and the Word was God. ² He was with God in the beginning. ³ All things were made through him. Nothing that has been made was made without him. ⁴ Life was in him, and that life was the light for all people. ⁵ The light shines in the darkness. But the darkness has not overcome the light. . .*

> *¹⁴ The Word became a human being. He made his home with us. We have seen his glory. It is the glory of the One and Only, who came from the Father. And the Word was full of grace and truth. [John 1:1-5; 14]*

Jesus came into this world so we could see God's glory. It is a gift to us to see his glory. It is like the gift of seeing the Grand Canyon, the stars in the sky, or the ocean—except that God's glory is a million times more fantastic. Even though we have lived in darkness, his light makes the darkness go away. Even if we have been separated from God by our drinking and drug use, Jesus joins us back together with God. He shines into the darkness of our lives and brings life and light to even the deadest, most spiritually isolated people. Therefore, I forgive you in the name of the Father, and of the Son, and of the Holy Spirit.

Everyone: Amen.

Facilitator Questions

What do you like about Jesus?

_____
_____
_____

Now that you are sober, what are you seeing that is worthy of your attention and praise?

_____
_____
_____

TREAT MYSELF WITH DIGNITY

Reader 1: (Scripture) *²⁶ Then God said, "Let us make human beings so that they are like us. Let them rule over the fish in the seas and the birds in the sky. Let them rule over the livestock and all the wild animals. And let them rule over all the creatures that move along the ground."*

²⁷ So God created human beings in his own likeness.
He created them to be like himself.
He created them as male and female. [Genesis 1:26-27]

Reader 2: Pedro looked terrible. He wasn't eating, drinking, sleeping, or exercising right. He didn't see the doctor when he needed to. His hygiene was lacking, his clothes were dirty and worn. The things under his care also looked terrible. His house was a mess. He had many unfinished projects. And most of his possessions were broken, lost, sold for cash, or stolen.

Although Pedro was created in God's image, he wasn't treating himself like he had any dignity or worth. He wasn't taking care of himself, much less taking care of the parts of God's creation that were under his care.

In treatment, he started to gain an awareness of his own dignity and worth as a human being. He also started to see that he had a role in taking care of God's creation through his work as a husband, father, and worker. So, he took better care of himself and his health. In fact, his health, safety, and dignity motivated him to stay sober.

Facilitator Questions

Did you treat yourself with kindness and dignity when you were drinking or using drugs?

_____
_____
_____

Did you do a good job taking care of things under your responsibility?

_____
_____
_____

Reader 3: We have confessed our sins to God and to each other. We admitted did not treat ourselves with dignity during our addiction. We've also admitted that we didn't take care of things under our responsibility. Let's take a moment to continue that confession in personal, silent prayer.

Reader 4: (Announcement of forgiveness, grace, and mercy) God cares for us. He created us with dignity and honor. Even though we have fallen and made a mess of things, he still loves us. The writer of Psalm 8 is amazed by God's treatment of us humans.

> *⁴ what is man that You are mindful of him,*
> *or the son of man that You care for him?*
>
> *⁵ You made him a little lower than the angels;*
> *You crowned him with glory and honor.*
>
> *⁶ You made him ruler of the works of Your hands;*
> *You have placed everything under his feet [Psalm 8:4-6]*

Through Jesus, God shows us how much he loves us. Jesus showed his love for us by becoming fully human. He gives us worth and dignity by becoming like us and dying to save us.

> *¹⁴ . . .So Jesus became human like them in order to die for them. By doing this, he could break the power of the devil. The devil is the one who rules over the kingdom of death. ¹⁵ Jesus could set people free who were afraid of death. All their lives they were held as slaves by that fear. ¹⁶ It is certainly Abraham's children that he helps. He doesn't help angels. ¹⁷ So he had to be made like people, fully human in every way. Then he could serve God as a kind and faithful high priest. And then he could pay for the sins of the people by dying for them. ¹⁸ He himself suffered when he was tempted. Now he is able to help others who are being tempted. [Hebrews 2:14-18]*

God made us. And when we sinned, he saved us through Jesus. No matter what we have done or how badly we messed up, there can be no doubt of his love and concern for us. Therefore, I forgive you all your sins in the name of the Father and of the Son and of the Holy Spirit.

Everyone: Amen

Facilitator Questions

How should we take care of ourselves?

_____
_____
_____

How should we treat other people caught in addiction or who relapse?

_____
_____
_____

MONEY AND ADDICTION

Reader 1: (Scripture) *[11]Money gained in the wrong way disappears.
But money gathered little by little grows. [Proverbs 13:11]*

> *[16]Those who do what is right may have very little.
> But it's better than the wealth of many sinners. [Psalms 37:16]*

> *[10]Love for money causes all kinds of evil. Some people want to get rich. They have
> wandered away from the faith. They have wounded themselves with many sorrows. [1
> Timothy 6:10]*

Reader 2: George loved money and he loved to party. He especially liked it when a party was
well stocked: overflowing with women, expensive booze, and pricey drugs. He liked the sense
of accomplishment and status he felt when everybody was drinking and getting high at one of
his parties.

But George hated his day job. The boss didn't pay him what he was worth, and he never
recognized George's hard work. The boss was also getting after George for stupid stuff like
little mistakes or showing up late. So, George turned to illegal activities to get the amount of
money he thought he deserved.

In rehab, George realized that he had almost no money left. He tried to do the math and figure
out where all his money went. But the numbers didn't add up. How could he have nothing at
the end of the day?

Facilitator Questions

Did drugs and alcohol help or hurt your financial situation?

_____
_____
_____

Were you a reliable and honest worker while using drugs and alcohol?

_____
_____
_____

Reader 3: We have confessed our sins to God and to each other. We admitted that drugs hurt
our financial situation. We've also admitted that we were not reliable or honest workers. Let's
take a moment to continue that confession in personal, silent prayer.

Reader 4: (Announcement of forgiveness, grace, and mercy) Jesus rejected the pursuit of earthly wealth. He sacrificed everything, never once choosing easy money, or corrupt paths.

His job was to live a perfect life and die a perfect death on our behalf. No one has ever worked so hard and been repaid so poorly for his labor. No one's work conditions have been so hostile and toxic. It was not easy for him to die for us. Knowing this, he prayed to be released from his work.

> *7 Jesus prayed while he lived on earth. He made his appeal with sincere cries and tears. He prayed to the God who could save him from death. God answered Jesus because he truly honored God. 8 Jesus was God's Son. But by suffering he learned what it means to obey. 9 In this way he was made perfect. Eternal salvation comes from him. He saves all those who obey him. [Hebrews 5:7-9]*

Jesus obeyed and completed his job—even though it was hard. Rather than celebrate the end of his work selfishly, he used his paycheck to clear all of our debts and —and then gifted us with eternal life in heaven. For all the times we wasted our money or were not good workers, Jesus forgives us and offers his perfect record to us like a robe to cover our sins. Therefore, I forgive you all your sins in the name of the Father and of the Son and of the Holy Spirit.

Everyone: Amen

Facilitator Questions

With gratitude toward Jesus, what kind of worker do you think God wants you to be?

_____

_____

_____

What are some God-pleasing ways to make and use money?

_____

_____

_____

FACILITATOR GUIDELINES

Allow people to pass. We want people to feel comfortable. Some people may feel more comfortable listening. You might worry that quiet people are disengaged, resistant, or not getting anything out of the group. If that is the case, keep in mind that people who do not answer are still getting many benefits from attending Resilient. They are voting with their feet. In other words, their attendance is a strong signal that they are considering or making a change. Silent people are also listening. They are processing the statements others are making and considering which statements hold value for them. Finally, silent people are choosing to spend time with a group of people committed to Christ and to sanctification. A Mexican proverb says this: "Tell me who you are with, and I will tell you who you are." So, we do not need to feel disappointed when people don't speak out loud in a meeting. Their presence in the meeting is still a blessing to them and to the rest of the group.

Get comfortable with silence. You might be concerned that pauses and silences after you ask a question are a bad sign. You might think that people are bored or unhappy about the group. In reality, there are many positive reasons that people pause before answering a question. First, they are thinking. The questions in this book are designed to promote introspection and self-examination. Introspection and self-examination take time. So, pauses are to be expected. Not only that but pauses should also be respected. A pause may be a sign that valuable thinking is going on. People could also be considering what to share. After they have performed the introspection and self-examination, they need to decide what to share with the group. Considering what to say takes time—and thus, it adds to the pause that happens before a person responds to the question.

Regardless of the reason for the pause, you are likely to feel panic and anxiety during the time between asking the question and receiving answers. Don't worry. It is normal. It is expected. Many times it is actually needed.

Repeat the questions. There are many good reasons why people would need to hear the questions repeated. For example, during the time of introspection and self-examination, the person used their cognitive calories for thinking—not for memorizing the question. When you repeat the question, you are helping them remember it. The same thing can happen when people are listening to another member share. People are paying attention to what the other member is saying. They are not memorizing the question. So, whenever a person finishes sharing, repeat the question.

Ask your own questions. There are times that even after getting comfortable with silence and repeating questions, a question bombs. You only receive silence in return. There are several reasons for that. **One,** the question might have been confusing. The author, who is certainly a genius among geniuses, is still a fallible human being. And sometimes he writes bad questions. I know it hurts to hear it. But Jason is just a man. **Two,** people may have thoughts about the question but do not want to share something embarrassing with the group. In that case, the question was good, and it promoted self-examination. But the group will not get to hear the outcome. That is fine. The person still got benefit from the experience. **Three**, the question is not applicable to their situation.

Regardless of the reason, you may rephrase the question. You are in charge, not the book. In fact, if you want to ask another question entirely, you may do that, as well.

Always respond to answers. Some members of the group may feel anxiety after they share. They may worry they are being judged. They may think they said something wrong, or embarrassing. Breaking the silence with a word of acceptance can reduce their fear that they are being judged. For example, just saying, "thank you for sharing that," can go a long way toward making the person feel safe and understood.

Paraphrasing a portion of a member's answer helps members feel comfortable. Paraphrasing validates the person who answered and shows that you heard them.

You can also share a summary of what the person said. This summary lets the person know they were heard. And it may prompt the person to introspect and share more. This second round of sharing may be more profound and nuanced than the first. Thus, you benefit the entire group.

Avoid correcting people. In Resilient, we recognize that you must catch a fish before you clean it. So, do not be surprised when your fish aren't ready for the plate just yet. This means that we welcome messy, unfinished people to Resilient. Often, members will have imperfect theology. They might lack wisdom in some areas related to their recovery. After all, everyone is a work in progress.

It can be challenging not to respond when we hear things we disagree with. But correcting people may have a stifling effect on a person. And correcting one person may have a chilling effect on others' willingness to share, too.

When dealing with the discomfort of listening to views we disagree with, it is helpful to remember the purpose of a Resilient Group. A Resilient Group is an environment where people confess their sins and hear the gospel message of forgiveness and reconciliation. It is more like a workshop than a showroom. Workshops are messy places. They are filled with scraps and failed experiments and prototypes. They look and sound nothing like showrooms.

Also, keep in mind that in addition to the person whose views you disagree with, there are 4 other influences in the room: 1) God's word, 2) the Holy Spirit, 3) the curriculum, and 4) other Christians. All these influences are actively at work. We can trust that over time that incorrect beliefs and statements will be ironed out. The truth will prevail.

Hold everyone's and no one's beliefs. Beyond just biting your tongue when you hear an error, try to model neutrality and acceptance. You do not have to endorse a belief to do this. In fact, you can accept two contrary beliefs and then solicit even more. For example, you may say, "Some of us are feeling like Jesus is frustrated with us when we relapse. Others think he is not. What are some more thoughts about this topic?" Another example is this, "Bob's goal is to moderate his drinking; Tom has 8 months sober, and his goal is to maintain total abstinence. What are some other goals we have?" Try to model acceptance for differing points of view.

By honoring each person's beliefs, you create a welcoming atmosphere. Our hope is that this safe, respectful atmosphere is one that pleases the Holy Spirit and allows him to work without our pride and ego interfering in his sacred business.

Avoid politics. It is wise to avoid politics in a Resilient Group. Politics is outward-facing, and Resilient is all about introspection and self-examination. People involved in a political discussion tend to focus on the sins of others and minimize their own sins and the sins of our political tribe. In contrast, Jesus says we should focus on our own sins and weaknesses.

> ³ "You look at the bit of sawdust in your friend's eye. But you pay no attention to the piece of wood in your own eye. ⁴ How can you say to your friend, 'Let me take the bit of sawdust out of your eye'? How can you say this while there is a piece of wood in your own eye? ⁵ You pretender! First take the piece of wood out of your own eye. Then you will be able to see clearly to take the bit of sawdust out of your friend's eye [Matthew 7:3-5]

I recognize that being apolitical is still a political stance. For example, being neutral may feel like opposition to the person who strongly believes that _____ lives matter. And this has real-world implications. By remaining neutral, I may be silent rather than speak up about evil. Neutrality can also prevent initiatives and laws in support of _____ lives matter from getting funded or passed.

But, the neutrality we advocate is only for the Resilient group itself, not for our lives outside the group. We elevate unity and acceptance in the group so that we can reach as many as possible.

> ¹⁹ I am free and don't belong to anyone. But I have made myself a slave to everyone. I do it to win as many as I can to Christ. ²⁰ To the Jews I became like a Jew. That was to win the Jews. To those under the law I became like one who was under the law. I did this even though I myself am not under the law. That was to win those under the law. ²¹ To those who don't have the law I became like one who doesn't have the law. I did this even though I am not free from God's law. I am under Christ's law. Now I can win those who don't have the law. ²² To those who are weak I became weak. That was to win the weak. I have become all things to all people. I have done this so that in all possible ways I might save some. ²³ I do all this because of the good news. And I want to share in its blessings. [1 Corinthians 9:19-23]

ABOUT THE AUTHOR

Jason Jonker is the founding director of Resilient Recovery Ministries. After a decade-long struggle with substance abuse and mental illness, he found relief in Christ. A former therapist and regional director for a non-profit mental health agency, he now finds joy and satisfaction in sharing Biblical wisdom and the gospel message with those in recovery. He is a college instructor on the topic of church-based ministries for mental health. He is also training to be a chaplain. Jason is married to Maria, and they have 3 adult daughters, all of whom live in Phoenix Arizona.

Made in the USA
Las Vegas, NV
06 December 2023

82208408R00057